Chickens in Africa

a memoir

Patrick (PJ), Anne, Lester, Patricia, Stephen
Chris (John), Alice, Donald, David

Chickens in Africa

A Memoir
Patricia Hernan Grube

With additional recollections by
John Grube, Donald Grube, Alice Christine Hughes,
David Grube, PJ Grube, Anne Grube,
Stephen Grube & Tim Donatelli

Cover and book design by Alice Christine Hughes
Cover art and illustrations by Donald Grube
Photographs by Lester and Patricia Grube
Photo editing by PJ Grube
Audio transcription by PJ Grube

Cover and book design by Alice Christine Hughes
Cover art and illustrations by Donald Grube
Photographs by Lester and Patricia Grube
Photo editing by PJ Grube
Audio transcription by PJ Grube

Printing by Community Printers, Santa Cruz

Chartreuse Publications
214 Sunset Ave, Santa Cruz, CA 95060

www. patriciagrube.com

ISBN 978-0-9726281-3-6

Forward

A few years ago I decided to write some short stories about a time in the early 70's when our family spent some time in Africa. It was just a few years after Zambia had gained independence from Britain. The effects of colonialism were still apparent. I have since verified in further studies some of my observations in a country newly free. The Zambia of today is very different from what it was when we were there.

The twelve stories I have written are true and some names are true, however several names are changed and some characters in the stories are composites of several people. I have fabricated the name of one company. The dialogue has been recreated even though the situations are true. Perhaps I need to say that my stories are "creative non-fiction". The main focus is of our family life in a new environment. Three people gave me letters I had written to them at the time. These helped me to unlock my memories.

When I gathered the stories together, I realized the book needed more. I asked each member of our family to write a memory. Chris, Donald, Alice, David and Patrick went to Zambia with us. Steve was working and Anne was in col-

"a group of friends who gathered together to talk about the world, the neighborhoods, our families and how we could contribute in each of these environments"

lege but they came once to visit and added their comments. David's friend, Tim Donatelli came to visit and has shared his memory. We were lucky to find a recording Lester made at that time, in which he describes the work he was doing.

Friends at home supported us in many ways, especially our mothers, my two sister-in-laws, Bonnie and Rosemary, and many friends. My sister Mary was a great help in doing all of our stateside business.

Donald's illustrations and Alice's use of them in her work of designing, add to the charm of the book. PJ has worked with the original negatives to prepare pictures for printing. The more we do the more we realize the importance of editors: thank you to Gail Brenner and Dina Hoffman who spent hours editing and proofreading the stories.

It takes more than writing to publish a book. Here, I want to thank Sioux Donatelli. We were having lunch one day when she offered to finance the project. Her folks, Mary and Gene Donatelli, have been our friends since the 50's. Their children and our children have grown up together. They were part of a group of friends who gathered together to talk about the world, the neighborhoods, our families and how we could contribute in each of these environments. Others were Esther and Joe Rechenmacher, Dolores and Sam Costanza and Terry and Bob Johnston.

Dedication

To our friends of many years
Mary and Gene Donatelli

Table of Contents

Index of Photographs

Before we left home we thought we would be
living in a mud hut with a grass roof.

How different this is. We're not even roughing it.

Here We Are: We Thought Things Would Be Different

Ndola, Zambia November, 1970

You'll be glad to know we are finally getting settled and looking for mail. Settled. This isn't exactly settled. I packed things so carefully at home. Remember? You helped me pack six wooden foot lockers. They haven't come yet. Our instructions were to send them by steamer. Now they tell us it might take another two months before the boat arrives in Mozambique. The port there is crowded. Zambia refuses to accept things coming through South Africa. I do agree with the embargo on South Africa but most of the Europeans here are furious." I was writing to a friend at home.

"Remember, before we left home we thought we would be living in the bush in a mud hut with a grass roof? How different this is. We're not even roughing it."

Every day I check for mail. There was one from our Real Estate Agent about selling the house and one from Mama who has not adjusted to our leaving. "What were you thinking, to do such a foolish thing. Those dear sweet children. I tremble to think what can happen in that primitive place."

Santa Cruz, California August 2013

As I think of that time now, I am in Santa Cruz, California, and it is August, 2013. We are well into a new century

and I am looking back to a time that was very different. I am trying to visualize things that happened many years ago. We were trying to plan our trip and to find information about life in Africa. What would it be like to live in the bush? Would we live in a grass hut? Would it be difficult to make friends if they didn't speak English? In 1970 there was no internet to help with research, and although I made many trips to the library to find out about Zambia, there was not much information: a few statistics on climate and some vague historical comments. From this distance it is even difficult to remember just why we wanted to go to Africa but I will try to write it as I see it now.

Years ago Lester and I joined a group of friends with common interests in the changes going on in the church and in the world. We were commited to improving our communities. Soon we were involved in efforts toward social justice.Together we became more and more concerned for the world our children would inherit. Each of the families in our group took on areas that matched their interest and expertise, be it church, town, country or world. We became involved in many activities that called for social change: civil rights of course, the farm labor movement, stopping the war in Vietnam. The 60s were a confusing time; there was a race to accumulate nuclear bombs, shelters were being built in backyards, good people were assasinated. Many of us joined protest marchers to express our dissatisfaction with many things. It was probably after a march in San Francisco protesting the war in Vietnam that we began to want a different kind of involvement.

We decided to try for an assignment in Africa. Lester had

spent several months teaching the elements of poultry husbandry to some Peace Corps volunteers who were going to India. We wanted to take our family with us to a developing country; we thought it would be a learning by doing experience for our children. Stephen and Anne were in college and would go on with that; the other five, Patrick, David, Alice, Donald and Chris would go with us. We were willing to live in whatever humble situation we would find ourselves.

After sending inquiries with resumés to seventeen countries, Lester received an offer to be the Provencial Poultry Officer on the Copper Belt in Zambia.

The contract with the government of Zambia was for two years. They would supply us with a place to live and a small salary for Lester that would cover our day to day expenses. The family was included under the same health insurance that covered the whole country. There were no additional perks as we were not supported in any way by any country or any organization. We would go just as ourselves.

As Zambia had gained independence only a few years before, jobs in companies and most of the government jobs were still held by colonials . Britain had not been concerned about education for Africans, so few were prepared to take over the many responsibilities. Neighborhoods in Ndola still appeared segregated although change was coming slowly as Zambians qualified for top level jobs that included housing.

On the morning of October 16, 1970, we left California for Zambia. As our tickets allowed unlimited stops we arranged to spend a month on the journey and visited Ireland, London, South of France, Rome, Athens and Israel.

When we arrived in Lusaka, the capital, we were met by

a government official, Lester's new boss, Peter Francis. He explained it would be a few weeks before we would receive the order to report to Ndola. Until then we were to stay in Lusaka at the Queen Victoria Hotel. Maybe that sounds like a vacation but with five kids needing to be amused with none of their friends, books, usual toys, and games and, of course, no TV, we were anxious to settle down. After a long month we drove to Ndola in our new Peugeot.

So many jumbled thoughts were going though my mind as I tried to write a letter to a friend, "Ndola, Zambia, December, 1970. We are finally in Africa. It's hard to believe we have a house after the long, long month in the hotel in Lusaka. If I never see the Queen Victoria Hotel again it will be too soon. It's just been a week since we drove here to Ndola, the capital of the Copperbelt Province. The border of the Congo is just a few miles away. All the houses are similar, stucco finish on cement. No wood because of termites. A wood frame house would be sawdust before the framing was done. The concrete floors are slick with several years of red wax build-up. There is a metal closet in the kitchen for storage. I can't get used to the burglar bars on the windows. How I wish we could sit down for coffee."

We had been assigned a house and had just moved into what would be our home for two years and I managed to make things attractive in a homey sort of way. At least I thought that was what I was doing. I stood by the window to survey the large yard, the jacaranda tree, the sturdy fence and the gate with a secure lock. A cement house is solid but cold. We needed pictures on the walls.

It's difficult to say how one really feels in a letter, but I tried to write frequent letters home to my mother and others and explain what our lives were like. Looking back now I am trying to summon up all those feelings of disconnection that come from being far away from home. Communication can now be instantaneous but in 1970 it was slow; almost two weeks for a letter to get to California and another ten days or so to get an answer. We didn't consider trying to communicate by telephone as it was difficult and expensive. After a while I found a typewriter when some folks were selling off their things because they were going home. Day after day I sat in front of that ancient typewriter trying to connect with those at home. I did get a lot of writing practice. Three people saved and gave my letters back to me and this has been a big help in reconstructing the adventure and some of my feelings.

Sometimes letters from home were disturbing. My best friend didn't seem to understand at all; she wrote, "After all the time we've spent together, you did this. You actually did leave. I thought we knew everything that was happening in each other's lives. We talked a lot about doing something different. I should have known you were serious. I keep trying to figure out why you left—it didn't seem like your kind of thing to do." When she wrote that they replaced me on the Parish Committee, even at that distance it was a jolt.

One day a neighbor invited us to spend the afternoon by her pool. The children loved to swim. I knew they would be excited. It was very relaxing for them and for me. Then she asked me a question, "What do you do, Pat?"

I had to think a while before I answered. "Me? What do I do? What I do is—well—there are the children, the house.

Oh, you mean do I have a contract to do something? —We believe that our whole family has the contract. We all feel we have come to help. I mean we are trying to teach the children about the world. This seemed a good way. I don't know. I want to do something. I'll be supporting Lester in his work. Of course–we came to–it seems like . . ."

I stopped trying to explain. I needed to think. Lester's work in the bush was going well. What am I doing? I was beginning to wonder what I do? It seemed that I was doing the same things I was doing at home.

Coffee in the Garden

At about ten o'clock one Saturday morning in Ndola, Zambia, Lester and I appeared at the gate of the Worthing home. The house inside the secure fence was similar to ours with the same kind of polished red concrete steps leading to the entrance of a beige colored stucco house with black burglar bars on the windows. Mr. Worthing was standing on the far side of the house in a patch of cabbages that looked as lovely as flowers. The house-boy had already placed a coffee service on a table in the formal flower garden. We knew he would hurry everything inside if a cloud appeared because this was the beginning of the season when heavy rain could come without any warning at all.

The houseboy opened the gate and indicated that Lester should join Mr. Worthing. After Mrs. Worthing's cordial greeting, I sat at the table and she poured me a welcome cup of coffee. I held the china up to the light to admire it. "Wedgwood?" I questioned, "Lovely."

She replied, "Mmm, oh yes, Mrs. Grube. We came here as settlers when I was a bride. John said this would be the place to make his fortune. All my wedding gifts. So many bundles and trunks and barrels and –Oh, my. It doesn't seem so long ago. I looked out the window of the train. All I could see was bush and all the bush looked like all the other bush."

I laughed, "When you've seen one bush, you've seen it all."

Her reverie seemed interrupted. "What, my dear?"

I laughed again, "When you've seen one bush, it's a kind

of joke; when you've seen one this, when you've seen one that—with hippos, or congressmen, or skyscrapers. When you've seen one mountain, when you've seen one river. Oh, it's what we're always saying. Well you get the idea. Our little joke. Do tell me more about when you came here."

She seemed eager to continue, "The train to Ndola was quite properly outfitted in those days. No one takes it now but Africans."

It was just a few months before, on a summer day in 1970, we decided to try for an assignment in Africa. Here we were in early December, having coffee in the garden and it was my opportunity to get information from a long time resident. "I'm making a list of things the children and I can do. The boys love trains and I do want them to experience everything."

She seemed shocked, "Oh, my dear, Mrs. Grube. The trains? You need to understand. It's not done. Crowded. Not clean. I would fear for ..."

I interrupted, "But, the children should—you know. I want them to experience the real Africa."

She seemed anxious to correct me, "Real? Your concept of real is naive. You'll learn, just as I have—just as we all have." She shook her head and went back to her story, "You were asking about the early days. We did come by train. Then, it was the only way." She smiled as she remembered. "As a bride. I looked out the window at the bush and as more and more bush was all I could see I began to weep. I had, until now, forgotten how I wept. John didn't understand but he took my hand and held it tight. I remember how he held his head, very straight. His face was rather grim. He looked out the window. He squeezed my hand and said, 'Althea, I didn't think there would be so much bush.'" She paused a minute, gently laughed, then slowly repeated, "I didn't think there would be so much bush." She leaned over to me and took my hand. "You are right, my dear. When you've seen one bush you've seen it all."

I put my hand over hers, "It's been a big help to talk with you. I was feeling quite alone. Lester is anxious to get started. He has been at so many meetings with the Provincial Officers making plans and, in between, of course, we've been getting the children into school. We were promised there would be places for them. But we didn't know they would be taking the places of African children. We didn't know places in school were so limited. I just hate that someone can't go to school because my child has taken their place. They promised us places but no one said it would be like this. They have to go to school."

"Well, of course," she replied, "You are being over concerned."

"We've taken them away from their country, their friends. They have to go to school."

"The government says they want to educate the African children." She explained, "You do understand they are quite unrealistic. Their goal was, by this year, to have every eight year old child in school. They are even bringing teachers from Tanzania in preference to our teachers from the UK. Can you believe that?"

This was my area of expertise so I jumped right in, "There are many things to learn in school–besides–learning. Teachers should be African. It's a role model thing."

Suddenly, Lester stood beside me and took my arm, "Mrs. Worthing, don't get Pat started on psychology." With a serious look in his eyes he said to me in almost a whisper, "No controversial subjects, Sweetie. Remember, you promised you wouldn't." Then he turned to the others, "What's your opinion, Mr. Worthing?"

Our host replied, "Education hasn't been a priority in this colony. With the British, all the emphasis was on the copper."

"Copper?" I questioned.

"Workers in the mines don't need an education." He said.

"The engineers? The managers?" I used my most judgmental voice.

He explained, "They came with their companies, British or American companies. Just six years ago this was a British colony. After independence, one of the first moves was to nationalize the mines. Kaunda thinks the Zambians can run them without our help. They'll have to show me. Can you believe the things that Kaunda expects. He has a plan for the mines and for the whole country to be self-sustaining in just a few years. Education takes time. But they have to prove first – that they can be educated."

I was astonished, "Mr. Worthing, you really can't mean what you are saying?"

Lester glared at me and tried to change the subject, "It's kind of Mrs. Worthing to extend this invitation after a chance meeting with Pat. And coffee? In the morning? Doesn't seem British."

Mr. Worthing smiled, "Oh, we know you Americans, how you do like your morning coffee. And we want you to feel at home. Rather nice custom: to chat over a cup of coffee.

When Althea said there were Americans in town, I was quite surprised. I am in touch, you know, as Provincial Manager for Imports/Exports and Travel. Althea said you are from California. I'm not aware of any American aid program with Zambia right now."

"Right. Mr. Worthing. We are not supported by any program. We applied directly to Lusaka."

"What is your story, Mr. Grube?"

"Protein." Lester continued, "Eggs. Poultry and eggs."

Mr. Worthing was surprised. "Poultry and eggs?"

Lester continued. "Protein. Well, that's the idea. Raising chickens. Protein. Eggs for protein."

Mr. Worthing wanted to show that he was on top of things, "I've been reading about new technology in egg production. 40,000 hens, each in a separate cage. Is it true their feet never touch the soil?" He chuckles, "My, my. Good luck in setting up your farm, Mr. Grube. You Californians think big."

"It's Lester. Just plain Les. John?"

"Yes, of course. Lester."

"And it's farms, John, lots of farms. If we can get some poultry farms started, it's easier and cheaper than, say, pigs or beef."

"Now, tell me, how does the government plan to finance all those cages? The chickens are going to live better than the Africans."

Lester laughed. "Oh, we're going back to basics. Just your small back yard flocks. Each farmer will have only a few hundred chickens. And the technology, the growing of chickens, is easy to learn. A brick enclosure. You've seen yourself, I'm sure, how they make bricks out of the soil from the ant hills? And they'll need some incubators. Those can be made of empty oil cans. No cages. Small flocks can be self-sustaining. The government is making small loans available; 500 kwachas can get a family started."

"It's true we don't get many eggs." Mr. Worthing said wistfully, "A few are imported from Rhodesia. Eggs are on the list of unessential items. They are very dear."

"There we go. I also have a marketing plan. Ndola will get eggs from rural areas right here on the Copperbelt."

"Marketing! That I understand. We don't get many Americans here. The Kingsleys left last week. Jolly fellow. Big American car. There have been a few others because of the copper. Engineers with the mines up in Lubumbashi and over in Luanshya. They left straight off when the mines were nationalized. Oh, yes, for a short time there was some farm aid from America. They cut off the program when the Chinese started building the railroad. I can show you some pretty fancy equipment sitting in the bush down by Mpongwe. Big devils. Broken down. Completely inoperative. Americans didn't have a program for sending *small* parts. Americans think big."

"It's a good story, Mr. Worthing. Believable. The ugly American story." Lester laughed.

I tried to relieve the tension, "Oh, Les, did you know they call cookies, 'biscuits' and biscuits, 'scones.'" I looked at Mrs. Worthing. "Do you have anything that you call 'cookies'? And when I was trying to buy paper napkins...first, I found out that they don't have many paper things here and when they do, they are very expensive. I tried to buy paper napkins. The clerk seemed shocked and then I found out that diapers are called napkins. It's as though English is a foreign language."

Mr. Worthing wanted information, which was the real reason we were invited to have coffee. "Jolly glad you could come this morning, Lester. I want to offer any assistance you might need in getting around, learning the ropes. Now tell me what brings you out here?"

Lester was eager to explain his mission. "Don't get me started again talking eggs. You see," he put his hands together almost in prayer, then gently opened them as if to offer Mr. Worthing an egg, "An egg is complete protein in a tiny globe. We are committed to this mission. We heard there was a need for protein. It's part of the plan to make eggs available to everyone."

Mr. Worthing frowned, "I don't think you can get the Africans to change their diets. What they eat is maize. The country runs on maize. It will be impossible to teach them anything different. The villagers all grow maize. They dry it and grind it."

I saw an opportunity to show off some of my new knowledge. "It's like corn meal mush! They boil it very thick and roll it in little balls. They eat it with their fingers! Isn't that it, Althea? Nshima !"

Lester turned back to Mr. Worthing, "Maize is also a component in feed for chickens." Lester held his hands up as if to cup an egg and said in a tone of wonder, "Like I said, don't get me started talking eggs."

"You do seem sincerely interested in poultry. Even though . . ."

"Even though?"

Mr. Worthing continued, "Don't misunderstand me . . ."

Lester was serious, "You see, John, we are committed to this mission. We heard there was a need for protein."

Mr. Worthing now revealed what was on his mind all along. "And the CIA?"

Lester was completely surprised. He exploded, "The CIA?"

Mr. Worthing lowered his voice. "Let me tell you a secret. Whether you are with the CIA or not, everyone will think that you are. We don't get many Americans here."

Mrs. Worthing got up which indicated time for us to go. She handed me the shawl I had tossed on the chair. As we walked toward the gate she issued another invitation. "Patricia come on Wednesday morning. You'll get acquainted with some of the other expatriate wives. We meet here in the garden and share recipes."

Les was very quiet but I sensed he was about to explode as he shook Mr. Worthing's hand and said, "We'll talk again. I'll be needing your approval for a shipment of chicks that will be coming soon from Rhodesia."

Wellington closed the gate behind us and we linked arms as we walked down the road toward our house that we hoped would soon feel like home. So much had happened since we left California. Now we were getting settled in a new place. It was not a hut in the bush but in a very nice house in a middle class neighborhood and we were beginning to make new friends.

Mr. Mbewe

The rainy season had just begun when our name came up for a telephone. Lack of one had added to our isolated feelings in a foreign land. Now we thought we would feel connected again although, who would call us? We didn't know anyone with a phone in Ndola. At least, I thought, my husband could let me know if he would be late coming home. Lester was working with the Provincial Government on a contract with Zambia to do rural development.

The first thing a neighbor told me was never to talk on the phone during the thunder storms which were sudden and presented a frightening electrical show. One afternoon a bolt of lightening blasted an old tree in our yard just before the boys walked in from school. There is more lightening on the Copperbelt Province than any other place in the world. Some people said they had first hand experience of lightening coming down the wires right into the house and knocking the phone out of their hand. To not talk on the phone during a storm may have been a modern day folk superstition but it seemed to have some basis in fact; as with most local customs we thought it best to go along with traditions. We hung up as soon as the rain would start; anyway, it was necessary to run outside and get the laundry off the line. In only a few minutes our few clothes would be wetter than when they were hung out in the hot African air.

It was a privilege to have a telephone. Right away we realized that Chris and Donald, the two youngest children, needed to learn some telephone etiquette. We did not want

CIA

them giving information to strangers. If a call came for the former owner of the number they would answer questions and sometimes begin to tell who we were and how we came to be there. "Yes, my Dad works here. Patrick and David go to the Kansengi Secondary School. Alice is in Form One at the sister's school. California–is . . ." As soon as we heard what he was saying we started "shushing" in angry tones and the little one would hang up in confusion. Then we would pull out all our own insecurities as we lectured on correct phone procedure.

None of us knew exactly why we felt ill at ease. None of us could define the problem, but living was more difficult than we had expected it to be. Most of the other ex-patriots were from the British Isles. We were the only Americans. Everyone we met was friendly and helpful but we felt that we had to prove ourselves. One person in a position of importance advised us in confidence that even if we were not with the CIA, people would think that we were. It seemed as though that was his way of letting us know that he was on to us.

Our number must have previously served a Mr. Mbewe (mmm-bay-way). As soon as the wires were connected we began to receive his calls. At first they were a diversion but as the days went by they didn't seem to slow down and sometimes would be downright disturbing. One day a woman insisted on talking to Mr. Mbewe. She would not believe he wasn't present and accused us of hiding him away. "I know that Mr. Mbewe is there," she demanded, "Put him on the line!"

We began to construct a picture of the mythical Mr. Mbewe. He was definitely connected with the police; but we were amazed that even his Captain didn't know he no longer had this number. He must be a dutiful son and brother, as family members would call hoping that we would finally give them a chance to communicate with him. He was probably the eldest son, as they would ask for him with great respect. He was without a doubt a trusted friend as some calls pleaded for us to tell them how to contact him as they needed his help. It seemed as though he must also be keeping another woman as we repeatedly received calls from someone who, when I would answer, would entreat me to leave her husband alone. You can understand why we were reluctant to have the children give out information. There might be recriminations.

As the days went by Chris and Donald learned to answer the telephone properly. Alice began to call her friend Fiona from the convent school to exchange confidences. Lester's work with the small poultry farmers was going well and he was establishing markets for their produce. I was learning to plan meals around what was available in the market rather than frustrating myself searching for favorite foods.

One day Patrick and David brought home a kitten whose antics began to take top billing over the phone calls. The kitten was almost completely black except for his feet, which were marked with low cut white boots. His coat was sleek and he had a dignified bearing. He would chase aluminum foil balls around the polished red cement floor, skidding in amazement where the wax was slickest. The cat acted as though he owned the place and we named him Mr. Mbewe. Now we were prepared to admit to anyone asking for him that, "Yes, indeed, Mr. Mbewe is here." Strange to say the calls stopped.

Mr. Mbewe

Animal Stories

#1

In Lusaka
the boys found geckos
on their walls in our hotel.
A lady from India said
to leave them alone,
"they'll clean the room of all
the little biting creatures."

#2

We had a house
in Ndola with a garden.
Chameleons
kept changing colors
as they climbed
brown branches
to hide in green leaves.

#3

The children left crumbs of cake
scattered here and there.
Too tired, I went to bed.
In the night grease ants
came in and cleaned the floor.

#4

In their separate kai in the backyard
David and Patrick had a monkey.
When he wouldn't be housebroken
even they became disgusted
and grudgingly gave him up.

#5

Donald found a cocoon
on a dry branch
and put it on the bookcase.
In the morning hundreds
of praying mantis spread
across the school books,
the novels and the family bible.

Soda Bread

By January our house in Ndola was beginning to feel like home. A note came from Mrs. Worthing inviting me to come on Wednesday morning to meet a few friends. I wanted to look my best so I wore my tailored slacks and a casual shirt. When I arrived at the gate I could see that several women were sitting at the table on the terrace and I was anxious to meet them.

The gate was locked. The house-boy came hurrying across the yard and I called out, "Good morning, Wellington."

He responded with the term of respect Africans use for a mature woman. "Good morning, Mama. I am presuming to ask a question, Mama?"

"Of course. What is it?" I asked as we walked.

"America very far away, Mama?"

"A long way. Yes, far away."

"I like to go to America. But, it give me great fright."

He seemed so concerned that I stopped to answer. "To travel is always a little scary. The garden here is lovely. You would love the gardens in California."

"Many gangsters! I very fright.'

"No, no, no, we don't have gangsters–well, we do have them. But they are . . .'"

"I very much do not like gangsters."

"Of course. But, really, there's no need to be scared."

"Madam is telling me that you be needing boy."

"Wellington, I have four boys, Patrick, David, Donald and Chris. I don't really need another boy." I laughed, "Oh! You mean a servant?"

"My brother will be coming to me. To work in city. He be much needing position. I will train him well, Mama."

So I tried to explain my own beliefs at the time. "We do our own work, Wellington. The children have their chores. Of course it's more difficult here without the appliances we are used to having. But we will do our own work. You see in the States, we just don't have servants. Of course there are some who do have servants. But, you see, generally, our custom is to do our own work. My belief is that we should not expect others to do our work for us. Nobody is better than anyone else in America. At least that's the idea. Just a couple of years ago our family–well, it's what we were marching about in Selma. It's been quite a while since Lincoln freed the slaves you know."

"Yes, Mama! I know Mr. Lincoln!"

Mrs. Worthing decided we had talked long enough and called out, "That will do now, Wellington."

"We'll talk again," I said.

He bowed to each of us and left. I put out my hand, "So nice to see you, Althea."

"My dear Patricia, come and meet the other wives. We have a regular United Nations here." We walked together to the table where the other women were waiting. "My dears, I want you to meet dear Patricia Grube from California. Patricia, this is Mildred Price. You must see her beautiful garden. She keeps three boys busy tending and planting. Mildred has two lovely children and her husband is with Deloitte, the accounting firm for the mines. They have been here four years from Johannesburg. She was born there." I thought it would be great to hear from somone who could tell me about the situation in South Africa.

"I'm so pleased to meet you, Mrs. Grube. My goodness, the United States! It is the most frightening place in the whole world to me. So much violence. Especially in California."

"Oh, no, Mrs. Price. Not at all. I hope I can change your mind about America. You sound so–your accent is very British?"

"My family came to Johannesburg many years ago from the UK."

Next I met Megan from Ireland and Althea explained. "Megan is a midwife. She has been doing first rate work. But with the upheaval in the hospital: one standard for all. It's one of Mr. Kaunda's unrealistic goals."

Megan told me how she was anxiously waiting for an assignment in Mapalwani Township. "The women want to have their babies near home. If the clinic will let me have one room for birthing. It's my dream." I was so impressed.

"Patricia, this is Ingrid Haller. She and Lars are going to Ngambi National Park to design a plan for Park Management. She is a Biologist."

"Yah, I am Biology. And Lars is an Ecologist. We are most excited to have this opportunity. We are anxious to be going to our assignment."

I took her hand, "I know how hard it is to wait. We've been doing our share of it. Waiting. Have you ever tried to amuse five children for a month in a hotel a mile from town, no car, no swimming pool? Nothing to do. The boys were making pets out of geckos."

We sat together at the table, Althea poured the tea; we

passed the cream and sugar to each other. Megan and Mildred wore print summer frocks and Ingrid a bright mini-skirt. I felt like a sparrow in my slacks and simple shirt.

Megan complemented Ingrid. "You look smashing, Ingrid."

"Yah, thank you, Megan. The rest of my wardrobe is all khaki and cotton, for Ngambi, the game park; it's more camouflage, more calm for animals. Soon we go. Lars is last day of orientation. Our house is ready. One year we are coming out and finally our house is ready. Lars, very patient. He says, 'We do our work soon. We need be more 'laid'."

Mildred was shocked, "My goodness! He said that?"

"Yah, is some American expression. 'Laid.' Something like that. Means relaxed, not so anxious."

Megan explained, "Oh! 'Laid back'. Be more laid back."

Mildlred went on, "Of course. It's 'laid back' not 'laid'. That's an American expression too, I think. It means— uh— you know. It's sexual, I think."

Everyone was laughing and Ingrid continued. "Yah. I think he meant that, as well. Is too much time we are having just waiting in the hotel."

Megan wanted to talk about her own situation. "It is difficult to wait. My assignment should come through soon for Mapalwani. I will be able to be near the mothers and help with some nutrition as well. For them and their toddlers. The children need so much."

Mildred put a piece of bread on her plate. "Is this your bread, Megan? Mmm – It's yummy."

"It's soda bread, Mildred. I make it whcn I feel a yearning to be home again."

"I know just what you mean." Althea said as if she had been dreaming.

At this point I noticed Mr. Worthing coming out of the house with Wellington, who is carrying a large knife. They go into the cabbage patch; Mr. Worthing points out a cabbage and goes back into the house. Wellington chops off the cabbage then he comes to the table and holds the cabbage out to me.

"Mama. Bwana is asking me to present this specimen of his garden to you."

"Thank you, Wellington. My family will enjoy the fresh cabbage."

Wellington tried again to convince me to take his brother as a houseboy. "My brother also a fine gardener. I shall teach him all manners that are necessary. Any problems–I am older and I will give discipline."

So I told him I would discuss the matter with my husband. He seemed satisfied with my answer even though I was quite sure I wouldn't be needing a houseboy.

I turned to the women again and discovered that Megan had an idea she wanted to share. "It's about the nutrition in the Township? Of course there is a need to help the women improve the nutrition for their families. I am trying to figure out how it can be done. While I am waiting maybe we can work out a plan. I think that together we can do something."

I mentioned that I have a hard time finding vegetables in the market. "We are tired of pumpkins."

Mildred said that is why she has a garden in order to have a variety of fresh vegetable. I asked her to show me how to make a garden. She explained, "With care many things will grow. Come 'round. An afternoon is best."

I still wanted to explain some of my hopes and dreams but Althea considered it as opportunity to instruct me. "I need to talk to you, Patricia, about the convent school. I can be of help to you in getting Alice into school with the Sisters. And I'm sure the other ladies will agree with me that little Chris needs to be in a nursery school. Mrs. Hunter, her school is the very best. If I ring her, you can be sure that the child will be placed, even though he is an American."

"What do you mean?" Mildred asked

"Oh, my dear, you'll have to agree American children are not well-behaved. They don't have manners, you know. Mrs. Hunter will start him out right."

At this point I was very annoyed but I tried to keep my composure and to be polite. "I wasn't planning to put Chris in a nursery school."

Althea continued. "And you must consider taking Wellington's brother as your house boy."

"Lightening hit this tree"

Ndola, Copperbelt Province, Zambia
January 1971

Lightening

It was time for the boys to come home from school and I was hoping they would be here before the rain. Suddenly, there was a flash of lightning with thunder right on top of it and a downpour so thick I couldn't see across the lawn. Almost at once Patrick and David came in the door. They were laughing and both wanted to talk at the same time. "It hit the tree!" They dripped water on the shiny red floor as they pulled me back to the window. It was true. The rain had stopped and wisps of steam were rising from the short black skeleton that had once been a tree in the front yard.

february

steam rises from the foliage
of the poinsettia trees
that will bloom at Easter

our boxes arrive from the states
smells from home
drift into the humid air

summer here is winter there
everything turned upside down
what's in these boxes that anyone needs

The Big Dipper

The kids had gone to bed and I sat thinking about the shipment of things that finally arrived from Mozambique. September seemed a long time ago when we had packed six wooden foot-lockers and sent them by steamer. Zambia wouldn't accept shipments from South Africa, so they were directed to the overcrowded port in Mozambique. By now I had forgotten what had been packed so carefully but it was kind of like Christmas to open them and find things we had learned to do without. Best of all was my sewing machine. Now we have some favorite books and games. We can use the extra clothes. Chris grabbed his favorite blanket. I am thinking that the kids will need the sweaters and jackets in a few months when the winter weather starts. I'll be happy to have my wool coat that was too bulky for the airplane. As we took things out and laid them around the room, smells from home drifted into the humid air.

Even though it was a hot summer night I put the coat around my shoulders and went to the window to look at the stars. I wish I knew something about them. I can identify the Southern Cross. Lester called me to bed, "Hey, Sweetie, it's an early morning tomorrow."

I was thinking that the moon was a connection with folks at home and if I look at the moon tonight, in 12 hours at home they'll be seeing the same moon but when I look at the stars–I called to him, "They're not the same stars."

"Of course they're not the same stars," he responded, "We're on the other side of the world in the Southern

Hemisphere."

I sighed, "I thought they would be the same." I continued looking at the night and there low on the horizon, I found the Big Dipper. That's all I've ever really been sure of—and—finding it—was like finding an old friend. It's here but it's not the same. I was sobbing as I called to him again, "It's not the same. It's not the same! The Big Dipper is upside down!"

"Honey—don't do this," he was standing beside me, "What difference if the Big Dipper's upside down?" He handed me a tissue, "Here—wipe your eyes, blow your nose. So the Big Dipper's upside down." He pulled me to the sofa and tried to change the subject, "How is Chris's knee?"

I sobbed again, "The doctor at the hospital today was Chinese."

"Chinese?" he questioned, "Don't tell me he gave Chris herbs."

I tried to explain, "The doctor was fine, but he was Chinese. I was surprised he was Chinese. Everything was fine. No, he didn't give him any herbs just some ointment for the sore on his leg. He said it would take a while for Chris to build up his natural resistance. Winter and summer are all backwards."

"I suppose it will." Les seemed pleased with himself.

I went on with the story. "It's so sad—the out-patient clinic. So crowded. Mothers and children, all of us, waited a long time in line. When the door opened we went in and sat in a big room together; the doctor and the children and about ten mothers all in the same big room. We watched each examination and heard each diagnosis. Today the doctor, the Chinese doctor was so kind. He was talking to a man, a man who was holding a very sick little boy—maybe three years old. A woman was translating what the doctor said into Cibemba. He told the man that his child had TB. The man nodded then just looked at his boy. His expression was so–resigned. Oh, Les. They wanted to put the child in the hospital. The man nodded to show he understood and then he just looked at his boy. All the mothers with their toddlers–and most of the women also had a baby on their back. They were all quiet, wondering, I think, about their own children. I know how I felt. We all felt the same–all of us felt the same–for the child–the man–for our own children."

He held out another tissue. "Hey–you'll make yourself sick if you go on like this."

I took the tissue and wiped my eyes, "You can say that, because you are really helping people."

Now he was now annoyed, "I have a long day tomorrow."

"Going out to the bush?" I asked.

"Come on, Pat, let's get some sleep," he put his arms around me.

"This neighborhood is all European." I said pulling away. "I had a nice chat today with a woman from Greece."

"From Greece?" He gave up, knowing he needed to listen.

"She invited me in. I was out walking with Chris. He played with her little boy in the yard while we had tea. She didn't know any English."

"You don't know any Greek," he began to get interested.

"We did a sort of sign language–about the kids and food– and–well, maybe it wasn't really a chat. I don't know."

He got up and took my hand. "Come on to bed, Pat. I do have to go to the bush tomorrow to meet some women who want to know about the chicken projects."

"You're out everyday." Then I put my problem into words. "I want to do something too."

"What about the group of women you get together with. Sharing recipes?"

"They're nice. We're getting to know each other. I do like them."

I had been happy to meet Mrs. Worthing, as she helped me to solve some of the problems of living and she had introduced me to some other expatriate women but that was part of the problem. Although I was happy to meet women from Sweden, Ireland and England, I really wanted to know some Zambian women.

Then he said, "You have the children."

With a little anger in my words, I said, "That's what Mrs. Worthing keeps saying when I ask her about things I could be doing here."

He began to laugh as I quickly said, "Don't you dare laugh."

He became serious and spoke sharply, "For god's sake, Sweetie. Loosen up. We've been here three months and you're freaking out."

At that I was angry. "How can you say that I'm freaking out?"

He pulled me up from the couch and put his arm around me. "This was your idea in the beginning. You expect too much too soon. Don't forget that you keep things together so I can do my work."

"I know that." I tried to speak calmly, "We were going to be a team but the kids and I see less of you than ever. Now–it doesn't seem like a team."

He pulled me close, "I need you Sweetie, you know that. Maybe we need some team building." I put my head on his shoulder and with his arms around me, we walked into the bedroom.

Groundnuts

In a letter to a good friend in California, I was writing about the weather. "We are finally beginning to understand the seasons although we are not yet acclimated to them. February, south of the equator, is the middle of summer, hot and wet. Everyday it rains. We hang the laundry on the line, then rush to take it down when the rain comes with no warning. Suddenly, the sun appears and we hang things out again."

"It is probably not possible to explain the drenching rain. There are deep ditches along the streets to carry off the sudden floods. Here is a story that may help to describe the intensity of the downflow. I was told that a woman sought privacy in a ditch in order to relieve herself; in so doing she was caught by the water and drowned."

"This is a bit of information you will like. I've been meeting with a group of women who have been cooking together. Deja vu? Remember when we would get together with Esther and Mary to plan the week, share recipes and do a lot of complaining? Everything changes and everything is still the same." I tucked the letter in my purse, planning to mail it on my way to meet with my new friends who are interested in nutrition.

As I arrived Megan was introducing a guest. "I brought Naomi Chipengo to tell us about the Township and the cooking methods the women use. She can give us some ideas about the best way to go about our project."

Naomi made a traditional bow that included each of us,

"You are very kind. Very generous ladies. I am pleased to meet with you."

We all sat down and Althea ladeled spoonfuls of beef stew into small bowls. Mildred had made it as a possible recipe we could present to the women in the Township. I commented, "This is very nice, Mildred. Rich, thick gravy."

Althea added, "The meat is quite tender."

Mildred was pleased with the praise, "It takes long slow cooking."

"It's hard to find good meat in the Butchery," I sighed.

Naomi said, "This is lovely."

Mildred was anxious to hear from Megan, "What do you think, Megan? It is nutritious, isn't it?"

Megan responded, "Yes indeed! These carrots and onions. Beautiful potatoes. The gravy is rich with boullion. There's no question about the nutrition."

"So will it do? As one of our first recipes?" Mildred beamed, "I want the women to really be impressed."

"Athough Ingrid's recipe for Swedish Meatballs was good, too." I continued, "My boys love Pot Roast. I can't find a good cut."

Mildred asked, "How are the children?"

I answered, "They're making friends. Getting used to the methods at school. Lots of things are difficult to understand. The ranking is strange to them."

Althea spoke sharply, "We've always had ranking."

Midred questioned, "What other way is there?"

I defended my point of view, "But in the third grade? Everyone in class ranked from 1-40. The top five are the– well–foreigners–but–because–the teaching is in English, not

Cibemba–so the children who grew up knowing English are bound to do better–so how can the competition be fair?"

Mildred looked confused, "What a curious thing to say."

Still on the defense, "I'm just saying what is logical. It's very–uh–well–not fair. My children aren't learning the lessons about life–the lessons I wanted them to learn."

Naomi entered the discussion, "My son, Peter, is very fortunate to be at the Kensengi school. He is busy learning and not thinking about 'fair'. So many children are not getting any education at all. He is grateful to be there. Peter tells me he is friends with your son, David. He tells me David was selected to be a Prefect and he declined. Why was that?"

Mildred was amazed, "That isn't done. One can't refuse that honor."

I defended him, "He didn't think it was an honor. He didn't want to be a policeman and 'rat on his friends.' Those were his words. His father asked him to reconsider."

Mildred was confused, "Rat? Rat on his friends? Whatever did he mean?"

I tried to explain, "This system of Prefects, and I must say they are mostly white, is even used in the Nursery School. This system is a not so subtle way of–continuing a division of classes."

Althea was shocked, "This is necessary for a well functioning society."

Trying to explain, "It becomes a caste system, so to speak. Part of the old colonial system."

Mildred exclaimed. "That's a curious thing to say."

I continued, "I'm glad that David didn't want to have a part in it."

Althea brought us back to order, "Ladies! We need to make this decision. Are we all agreed? Shall we choose Mildred's beef stew? And, Mildred, will you do the first demonstration? Megan can describe how the stew is good nutrition for growing children. Patricia and I will pass out samples for the women to taste. We can use little nut cups and wooden ice cream spoons. Naomi's job can be to translate everthing into Cibemba."

Mildred continued, "Yes. I am pleased to do the demonstration. And none of us speak Cibemba. So we really do need you, Naomi, to translate."

Naomi asked, "You have seen the charcoal burners. For use in cooking?"

Mildred added, "Here in town, too. The servants cook their meals on charcoal in the back garden in front of their kai."

Althea chimed in, "Oh, yes, we've all seen the charcoal stoves."

Mildred asked, "What about the stew? Could we cook it on the charcoal fire?"

I mused, "I don't think I could squat so long. My legs ache just thinking about it. Could we put the charcoal burner on a table?"

Naomi continued her story. "Our market. Not always having potatoes. Sometimes potatoes. The marketeers hold their prices very tight. We would much like to have potatoes."

Mildred was disturbed, "Potatoes? No potatoes? Potatoes are essential for my stew!"

Naomi continues, "In our Butchery. Meat is very dear. Some meat. But very dear."

Mildred draws a conclusion. "Then you are saying that the stew isn't really practical. Is that it, Naomi? Megan? Is that it?"

Naomi explains, "We cook the maize and make nshima. If you come to my house this week. I will make some nice sauce for nshima. Sauce of groundnuts. Another sauce, kapenta. Both much protein."

I wanted more information, "Isn't kapenta those small fish–kind of like sardines, but all dried up? They come from Lake Tanganyika."

Naomi responds, "Megan is teaching me about protein. Also about vitamin C. We have mangos. Good vitamin C." She continued to tell us more about the township and the women there. Then we all agreed to meet the following Wednesday morning at Naomi's house. Although I was looking forward to that, I felt disturbed about our seemingly unsuccessful meeting.

As I walked into the garden, I saw Lester at the gate as he called out to Mr. Worthing. "Came to get Patricia. Looks like I'm right on time."

I heard Mr. Worthing respond, "Oh, this sharing of recipes is getting out of hand. It used to keep Althea busy and out of trouble. Now, I'm suspecting it means trouble. And your wife is at the center of it."

Lester tried to defend me, "Pat gets lonely. She's busy taking care of the children but I'm gone a lot visiting farmers in the bush. I'm glad that Althea has taken Pat under her wing. She needs feminine companionship."

"Yes. The dear ladies do need companionship." Mr. Worthing said as the men wandered over to where we were saying our goodbyes.

As Lester and I walked toward the car I saw the clouds gathering and hoped we would be home before lightning broke open the sky.

* * * * * * *

It was evening. I was sitting by the window, dreaming when Lester came in, bent down and kissed my neck. Without turning I said, "You seem very satisfied with yourself tonight? Things must be going well."

"Yeah." He continued, "The farms are working out. The chicks are arriving in good shape. Six more farmers are ready to go. Their chicken houses are finished to the government specifications and they have their applications in for loans. I'm meeting a plane tomorrow to pick up a shipment."

"I'm needing some help from you." I said,

"Althea's houseboy has a brother who needs a position. He'd rather have a family than work at the hotel."

"You know how I feel about having servants."

"You can't have it both ways"

"But it brings a class system into my own house. One day I had Mildred's garden boy come to help with the lawns. I gave him lunch with the children and me. He told Mildred he thought we were strange and didn't know how to treat servants. He wouldn't come back."

"There's not much I can do but I hope you change your mind." He responded. "I'll take the boys fishing next weekend. Mr. Kaliwands told me about a great place".

"Things are so easy for you. You see a problem; you solve a problem. Things are more confusing than all that; to me, anyway. I see muddle and trouble and want to jump right in.

When I do it just gets more muddled."

"John thinks you're meddling."

"I'm never anywhere to do any meddling."

"The wives. Expressing your idealistic views to them."

"So now I can't talk to anyone but kids?"

"I told John I would speak to you."

"So now you've spoken."

"Changes come slowly."

"So I have heard!"

"So you will cool it? Sweetie–just a bit?"

"You can tell John you spoke to me."

He leaned over to kiss me then pulled away, "We are a cold fish tonight."

"Be realistic, Lester."

Under the Slave Tree

Tired and hot I found a shady spot
in the south-east section of town
beneath a tree with a plaque which
read, *auctions were held here.*

We were looking for an Indian Store
whose proprietor mixes fresh curry.
Our neighbor said he would have garlic.
We were hungry for garlic.

My brother says we have no black blood
but I learned our ancestors owned slaves.
I read a will bequeathing them
along with land, to favorite sons.

The Congo is just across the border.
It's a long trek straight west to the coast.
Looking for some shade, I found a tree.
It seemed that I had been there in the past.

Chicks

Lester opened the gate and walked directly to the cabbage patch where Mr. Worthing was giving instructions to Wellington. Only remnants of old plants remained. It was June and winter had begun. Mr. Worthing turned and came across the garden, hand out stretched, and Lester called out. "I thought I could find you in the garden."

"Lester, so good of you to stop by." Then he said to his houseboy, "Wellington, we'll have tea out here."

"You know why I'm here, John." Lester was obviously upset as he walked toward the garden table.

"Sit down, Lester, it has been a busy day. Suddenly it's winter weather; June is always cold. Cold and dry. My old bones feel it." Then he called to Wellington, "Tell Madam that Mr. Grube is here. And do bring a cardigan."

Lester replied. "The seasons may be upside down but other things really piss me off!"

John seemed surprised, "Oh?"

"My shipment from Rhodesia." Lester's temperature was rising. "They were bumped in Lusaka for some lousy grapes. Grapes for the European community!"

"Oh my," John feigned surprise.

"We were promised a priority number." Lester accused him directly.

"The request was going through channels." John explained. "Lester, you should take this matter up in my office. It's not my custom to do business at home. A man's home is his castle."

Lester continued, "Day old chicks can't survive such treatment. Forty per cent are dead and those left have only a fifty percent chance of survival. Two thousand babies!"

"Now, Lester. This has to be disappointing."

"Disappointing? It's disastrous. It's murder!!"

"Now, now–that's a strong accusation."

"Six rural families in my first demonstration group. Each in debt for 500 kwachas! Cash borrowed to prepare pens and coops. I promised they would easily make it back at a good rate. Each one was to have 300 baby chicks. Now, only a few chicks will pull through. They can't make enough to pay their loans! Five hundred kwachas may not be much to you, John, but it's a fortune to a rural family."

Mr. Worthing paced his words. "Lester, I advised you early on to take it slowly. You Americans want everything to happen day before yesterday. You need to develop some patience. Get into the African rhythm."

"Africans didn't invent the bureaucracy and develop red tape to the fine-tuned colonial system that you maintain, John!"

Wellington brought the tea, set it on the table and put a cardigan on Mr. Worthing's shoulders. Lester was pacing. Wellington left.

"You need to know about chickens." Lester emphsized his points by counting and pointing with his fingers. "First. When the eggs go into the incubator the countdown starts. Everything has to be ready–to get them to their destination and everything has to move quickly when they are hatched. You need to realize that when the chick comes out of the egg there is enough yolk to nurture it for a short time. A short time. Maybe two days. And they begin to dehydrate very quickly. They must have water soon. One day we'll have a hatchery here but now we have to rely on Alitalia air freight and you."

"Now, Lester, sit down and have some tea."

Lester reluctantly sat down and took the cup. "We will be shipping two thousand more chicks in three weeks. I want your promise. Your solemn promise and a high priority number."

"You will need to develop some flexibility–to get on here. When I first came out, I was with the mines. Young, impatient. But you Americans have it over everyone in that department. Getting things done, an absolute obsession with you Yanks. There are certain ways of doing things."

Lester stood up, "We know red tape when we see it."

Mr.Worthing stood up. "Progress isn't made with threats. No, not at all! You will come to the office and we will settle this matter there. Wellington, come and show Mr. Grube to the gate."

A Sauce of Pumpkin Leaves

Ndola, Zambia, September, 1971

It's September and the jacarandas are in bloom–really fantastic–they look like wisteria except for being huge trees. There are still blossoms on the bougainvillea vine that covers the fence and in some places they have climbed up tall trees that become full of dark purple or red blossoms. Everyone is getting ready for rain. The ground has been prepared and maize has been planted on high rows beside deep channels so the heavy downpour won't wash out the seeds. It all needs to be ready as soon as moisture appears.

My friend, Sara has been asked to talk to the parish club back home and she wants to talk about our experience in Africa. We have been here almost a year and I am trying to think of information that they might find interesting. I've already written in other letters about the upside down seasons: summer, wet and hot, when it is winter at home; winter, cold and dry, when it is summer at home. "Sara, I will give you a bit of this and that and you'll have to pick out what you like best."

I poured myself a cup of coffee. I began to think about several experiences Sara might find interesting. So I started to write again, "I'm not sure, Sara, what aspects of life the women will want to hear. I suppose they will be interested in food and the difficulties I have planning meals. Well, it depends from day to day on what is available. There are usually bananas and oranges. Papayas will soon be in season

and mangos will be ripe by Thanksgiving. Although there are lots of pumpkins and cabbage, I have to rely on canned food. Corned beef in cans comes from Argentina and there is almost always Spam on the shelves. Remember how we depended on Spam during the war? I wrote before about the flour shortage. We always have maize so I made corn tortillas from a recipe that Mama sent."

"Avocado trees in our yard are loaded; they are as big as grapefruit. We have plenty to eat and give away. Last season two women came to the gate and asked for some of the fruit. They filled two huge burlap bags. With babies on their backs and the bags on their heads they walked regally toward the gate. When Lester saw them with the heavy loads he offered them a ride to their home, several miles away. The older woman sells the avocadoes for 5 or 10 ngwe each at the township market."

"Last Sunday we went to an Agricultural Fair in a rural village. I was taking pictures and a kind old man with very white hair pushed me into an opening in the crowd. He seemed anxious for me to see what was happening. A woman was dancing and a man with a drum accompanied her. Soon I realized she was dancing out the story of birth—even before conception. It was so intimate, that it didn't seem right to use my camera. The audience was caught up in the emotion of the dancer as if they themselves were experiencing every pang of labor. "

"I think I wrote to you before about the few days that I spent in the hospital. Included in our contract with Zambia was coverage for the family under the National Health Insurance program. My neighbor advised me to go to a private hospital instead of the government hospital, but as usual I wanted to do it my way. I couldn't speak Cibemba, but in the large ward the women and I smiled at each other and in our common suffering seemed to communicate. The lady next to me was middle-aged and I think she must have been someone important in her village. When the door opened at twelve for the visiting hour, eleven men came in and stood around her bed. They came in silently and greeted her with a clap-clap of the hands, then touched their hearts. Their motions were full of feeling. They looked closely and respect-fully at the bottle of plasma and their eyes followed the tube, which connected with her arm. No words were exchanged. I don't know whether they were persons who in ordinary life would not have conversed or whether they were awed with the power of the modern *mutei*. (The word for medicine is the same as the word for tree.) When the time was up they left silently. Somehow this conveyed to me their deep feel-ing of respect for the lady in the bed. Even more, it seemed to show their awe for the life and death processes that were happening."

"The Nutrition Group is going well. These are the women I met when we first came here. I think I wrote to you about them. We go twice a week to the Itawa clinic on the outskirts of Ndola. First we give a short presentation about some basic diet need followed by cooking something over a charcoal burner. Then we sell whatever we have brought. The time set aside for examination of pre-school children is the best time to contact mothers in order to sell small packets of dried fish, milk biscuits, groundnuts, dried beans and milk pow-der. Sometimes tinned meats and fish are available. Lester is able to provide us with eggs because of his work with poultry farmers. There is such a demand for eggs that we have to limit the purchases to one dozen each."

"This Wednesday when the group met to make plans we actually cooked some African food. Naomi is a Zambian woman who invited us to her house and helped us make a recipe of pumpkin leaves and groundnuts. The leaves were coarsely chopped and the nuts were pounded very fine like flour. She added just a bit of onion and a small tomato for seasoning. She simmered it all together with water until it was the consistency of gravy. Very delicious. She served it with Nshima, which is a thick, maize-meal porridge. Naomi is going to help us have more realistic plans when we go to the Township. She taught us the word 'mutende.' It means peace".

"Naomi is someone who really acts on her convictions. Recently she met with some local women in the Township to protest the unfair practices in the markets. They are going to march. She said she had heard about Selma and Dr. King. She told me they plan to carry brooms and pots and pans and shake them furiously at the marketers. And, they will march bare-breasted as a symbol of their motherhood and concern for their children. The bare breasts are a traditional sign of deep unhappiness. They will march next week. She hopes there'll be at least fifty women, maybe more."

"I'll sign off, Sara, and hope this will help with your talk. Of course most of my time is taken up with the usual stuff around the house. Everything is dusty and dry but they say the rains will start soon."

Dancing the story of life

Why Green Mango Pie

The seventy tribes of Zambia
free from Britain's colonial rule
now needed help and people came
from Scandinavia and Ireland
from Kenya and South Africa.

There were Scots, Chinese, Canadians,
Greeks and Portuguese. We were there
with five children who were always
asking questions. "Who was Guy Fawkes?"
"Why do the dogs bark all night long?"

In the market, vegetables and fruit
were scarce. Cabbage, pumpkin, papaw
groundnuts, avocado, maize,
sometimes carrots and plantains.
The man at the butchery wiped

his hands on his apron and said
"There will be no turkeys, maybe lamb
from New Zealand. Maybe Danish ham."
We had to learn to improvise
with Curry and Nshima. Pumpkin soup.

"Mango pie" my neighbor said to me
"will taste like apple you will see."
Tart fruit, carved from the thready pit
cut green not ripe, about a quart of it.
The crust was flaky, crisp and light

filled with mangos and browned just right.
We gathered together and prayed
then after dinner we all agreed
"It's just like Grandma made."
When we ate green mango pie.

Time is Relative

Ndola, Zambia, November, 1971

The rains have come and with them, sore throats, colds, runny eyes and tummy aches. I keep hoping that everyone will get well all at once. The rains have also brought out flying ants, beetles and lots of other little creatures. So glad we have the ducks; they are becoming less vegetarian. Vegetables grow like mad but bugs are right there to eat them up. Right now the sun is shining and I hope the clothes will be dry before another shower.

I poured myself a cup of coffee, looked at the empty chair by the table and wished my friend Sara were sitting here with me for a morning of gossip. She sends me news clippings and it's good to stay in touch with things but I get homesick. At least I can write to her so I continued a letter I started yesterday. "The children are now on holiday. I like this schedule–in school for three months, out for three or four weeks and then back again to school. We don't get nearly so tired of each other and the kids don't forget what they've learned. They don't have to play catch-up when they return. It seems odd, but it works."

"Alice seems to have an easy time making friends. She met Fiona Condon at school. They walk home together as the family lives in the neighborhood. We invited her family for Sunday dinner a few weeks ago. Everybody, including Chris, took turns playing Badminton. Great Fun! They invited us to their house next week. Both of them teach school and are

very British. Alice is getting a British accent even though the nuns at the convent school are German."

"It seems as though we were the only people in Ndola to celebrate Thanksgiving. There were orchids on the table; three stocks of orchids–five to nine blossoms on each stem. We found them in the bush when we took a drive."

"I couldn't find a turkey anywhere, except for one that was all dried up from being poorly wrapped in a freezer for such a long time. So the menu was: chili beans, tortillas and some nice salads. We invited Mildred's family, Naomi's family and the Condons. Mildred said, 'This is just like I imagined California would be.' David started to tell about the first Thanksgiving. Mildred said she knew the history of California and how the Indians and the Spanish were there first and she thought this was a 'beautiful tradition.'"

"So who needs turkey? For dessert, I made a green mango pie. I put in a lot of cinnamon and it tasted almost like apple. I used the last of my flour on the pie. There is none in the stores. The bakers get some flour but bread is available only occasionally. They use much of their flour for cakes and other goodies, which have no price control (as bread does). It reminds me of Maria Antoinette saying, 'Let them eat cakes.'"

"Thanksgiving marks a year since we've been here. Last year we had to do with a regular meal at the Victoria Hotel. That was shortly after we had arrived in Zambia and it seems a long time ago. But it's just a year. I'm already starting to count the days. Everything seems much slower now like it did when we were kids waiting for something to happen. Remember how hard it was to wait. Time is relative. It seems as though we've been here a very long time."

I picked up a bundle of letters from Ruth who is looking for new renters for our house. She says not to worry she will take care of everything but I am uneasy. Managing things from this side of the world is difficult. We knew when we left that it would be hard to live on the stipend from Zambia. When sponsored by a country, they give added perks to make up the difference, but we came on our own. I guess we've always been do-it-your-selfers. Ruth suggests that we get an equity loan on the house to see us through. "Pat, I am waiting for you to send the application for the equity loan on your home. Please have Lester fill out the section labeled 'Primary Borrower.' Put your information in the next section as 'His Wife.'"

Here are those applications for the loan and the directions. Once again Lester's signature goes on the first line, mine on the second. I think my name should go on the first line, I pay all the bills. Oh well, I'll get Les to sign tonight.

Then came a note from Father Martin, the parish priest, "The men's club has nominated Lester for the Diocesan Peace on Earth award. How proud you must be, my child. Behind every great man is a good woman, they say, and I do believe that it is true. God's blessings on you and your family."

I wrote to Father Martin to tell him how pleased Lester was with the good thoughts of the men's club. I boldly mentioned some things I had been thinking about and he responded, "Your concept of God has some relevance. Theologically– God does embrace both the masculine principal and the feminine principal. We have always recognized the feminine in our Holy Mother Church and Our Blessed Mother Mary. Listen to your heart, child. The spirit is always there if we listen."

One does have lots of time to think about things so I continued sharing some of my thoughts. He replied, "Your comments on theology are valid, but after all, this is only intellectual. It is the spiritual we must be concerned with. There is the question of 'Obedience' and 'Humility.' I advise them for your meditation."

In the same mail was a letter from Ruth saying, "The Title Company needs an Identity Statement from you, Pat. A form is enclosed. They will need your answers to all the questions. Be sure to include your father's name and that of any former husband so they can decide who you are." I guess that's the whole point in life: to find out who am I.

When we were bird watching, I was fascinated by the whydah—it's black and white and the male has a tail, four times as long as he is. When he flies, he sort of bounces. It's funny to watch him bouncing around, showing off his fine tail. This business of "men this" and "women that" is really getting to me.

Jobs

Ndola, Zambia, June, 1972

Lester was calling for the third time for me to close my book, that it was time for bed. He came in and put his arm around me. "Penny for your thoughts. Or maybe I should say a kwacha?"

I laughed, "A kwacha is too much. That's more than a dollar."

"Your thoughts must be at least worth that!" He kissed my neck.

I turned around to face him. "Do you think Mama's well?"

"What does she say?"

"Just things like, 'Don't worry about me.' or 'I'm feeling fine this week.' It's very suspicious. I'm so glad, Honey, that we'll be going home in a few months. I can't believe it."

"I suppose you're right, Babe. We do need to think about it." Lester pulled me into the lounge chair.

It felt good to be close. It felt good to start making plans. "Our renters need to be notified. I'll tell Ruth to handle that. But finding a job might not be easy. Of course Mr. Leach wants you to teach at Cal Poly, but San Luis Obispo is a long way from our friends in San Jose. We can start working on your resume now and start sending out some letters."

"I already have several offers." He felt me pulling away and he pulled me back, "Pretty solid offers. I was waiting a while to tell you."

"Waiting? Why?" I jumped up. "What's it about? Tell me

now."

He spoke slowly, "I wanted all the details. They are important for you to see the advantages."

I sunk down in a chair, "Why, Lester? What details? Tell me now."

"Mr. Kaliwanda wants to build and expand. Then we wouldn't need to have chicks shipped from Rhodesia."

"Of course I know, Mr. Kaliwanda, you have helped with his hatchery." I was beginning to understand, and slowly beginning to be more and more alarmed. "He wants you—oh, Lester!"

"He has a large acreage and would build a very nice place for us."

"Way out there on that bumpy road. The only schools are here in town."

"That's another thing to talk about. I wanted to tell you after I had more details."

I felt the blood rushing to my face and could hear my heart beating faster as I tried to control my anger. "You have everything figured out?"

"I knew, Babe, that you would have a problem with this. Because you get ideas. Ideas that are not flexible."

"Ideas? I thought they were our ideals!" I responded.

"Call them what you will." He was trying to calm me down. "You accuse me of abandoning our ideals. I've done what we came here to do. I introduced poultry husbandry to the new agricultural school. I developed a marketing plan. I trained Mr. Chishimba to take my place as Provincial Poultry Officer. That doesn't even include the many small farms in the bush."

"And what about Mr. Wilson? You helped him establish a large poultry farm."

"He has the same rights as any other citizen. When he left Southern Rhodesia he became a citizen of Zambia. He saw the way things were headed and didn't want to be caught in a revolution. By the way he invited us to a big 'do' he is planning next weekend. We need to make friends with . . ."

"I'm not interested in Mr. Wilson's 'do'."

"Please think about these opportunities, Pat."

"Just when had you planned to let me in on these opportunities? It's hard to see how there could be advantages."

"I wanted to present it all at once, so you would see the benefits. For one thing, the kids could go to excellent schools in England."

"The kids in England!" I exploded, "My god, Lester, I don't think I know you any more. What are you thinking?"

"I'm thinking about the kids getting a good education. You've seen how this works. Every few months they would come home for holidays and school leave."

"I'm not going to send my kids off to England."

"—and you would have time to–you know–do–things. You would be free to continue your work with Megan in the Township. That is going so well. You've complained more than once that you are just doing housework. How many times have you said that you came here to do something. You would have the opportunity to do things you have talked about. Meaningful work."

"Meaningful work! I already do meaningful work. Perhaps you haven't noticed. The kids are learning more here. Just being here. Their idea of the world has grown in a different way than at home."

"So now, Pat, you tell me that you are satisfied?"

"In some ways I've gained a lot but I'm ready to make plans to go home."

"You need to know that I am seriously looking into this job offer with Mr. K."

"I am seriously thinking it's time to go home and forget about saving the world. I don't want to fall into a pattern of life like those old time colonials."

"You can certainly push pins into a fellow's opportunities. I don't want to pass up a chance to make a good living. Think about it, Pat. I've looked into this from every angle. Mr. Kaliwanda is well respected."

I held back my tears. "Hold me, Les. Hold me. My world is falling apart." He put his arms around me.

* * * * * *

A few days later I wrote a letter to Sara and included this information. "The end of the contract extends into October. The kids and I have booked a flight for the end of July when the school year ends. Hopefully, Lester will finish his work quicker without us here. Maybe a few months. We'll see what happens then."

I sealed the envelope just as Lester came in. "The kids are asleep. Chris dropped off before I finished reading." He kissed my neck. "I love you, Babe."

"And I love you."

Then he asked me, "What is that word you are always saying? It means 'peace'?"

"Mutende."

He replied, "Mutende."

I didn't know.

Before I went to Africa I didn't know
much about giraffes. I made a little movie
of them at the zoo. Noble creatures
with long necks and tiny heads.
I didn't know that natural selection
designed their uncoordinated structures
so they could eat the tender leaves
at the top and leave the tree to thrive?

Before I went to Africa I didn't know
that elephants in the zoo were different
from those in India. It's in the ears?
I didn't know that an elephant,
with big ears flapping in the air
as it charges out of the bush
down the path toward our car
would be a frightening thing.

Getting Through Customs

Los Angeles, California August 1972

We were headed for San Francisco but first we had to clear customs at LAX. The line was long and the children were impatient and tired, yet excited to be back in the United States. Two years can be a long time. In 1972 the system was quite simple: just rollers on long tables to move our boxes, luggage and individual small private cases containing each child's treasures. It was our turn and the official with a stern face and a big badge looked at our assortment.

It would be a challenge to go through everything and we wondered where he would begin. We could see that the bags of the passengers in front of us in line were being closely examined even exposing their personal items. We tried to be patient as we waited for him to begin.

Chris was fidgeting and reached for my hand. Alice was serious as she watched. Donald put his hand on his small case as if to protect it. After a minute, which seemed like an hour, the customs official began by asking where we had been and how long we had been gone.

I said, "We've been in Zambia for almost two years. My husband is stationed in Ndola and has six more months of duty. It was necessary for us to return early."

"Now, to examine your bags," he said as he eyed everything. I wondered how I would be able to repack the boxes, which were bulging and held together with strong twine tied in tight knots. The man reached for Donald's case and

Donald reluctantly removed his hand. The catch released easily and as the lid was raised, feathers floated into the air.

An astonished look flashed on the man's face as he quickly closed the case, engaging the catch. He smiled at Donald. Then he signed a paper and handed it to me. In a stern authoritative voice, "You can pass on." A few feathers floated above our luggage as it rolled down the long table.

Culture Shock

Santa Cruz, California, September 1972

I walked into the produce department at Safeway and stopped right in the middle to look around at the vegetables: green and red cabbage, celery, cucumbers, carrots, beets and at least four kinds of lettuce. In a six by six bin tomatoes were piled in mountains, big fat beefsteak tomatoes and little pear-shaped Italian tomatoes. Another bin held zucchini, lovely matched sizes with not a single wormhole. I picked up pieces at random and looked for yellowing flesh and tell tale holes, tiny pin-prick holes that are made by worms or insects. I found none.

There were piles of potatoes, white baking potatoes, smooth and round, also onions of every color and there was a whole bin of garlic, fat and pungent. Garlicky, oniony smells and the musky smell of potatoes blended with the moist spray that the clerk was using to freshen everything.

I looked in another direction and saw oranges, grapefruit, tangerines and lemons. There were avocadoes that seemed tiny compared to the large ones that grew on the trees in our back yard in Zambia. The ones I remembered were the size of grapefruit. We used them in everything and gave them to anyone who wanted them.

As I stood there in the middle of such abundance, I remembered my search for garlic. As soon as we were settled in a house and cooking our own meals we wanted the food we were accustomed to. After a month in a hotel, with

a diet of bland British food, we were hungry for garlic. I finally found some in an Indian store that had a small supply. The proprietor put most of what he was able to get into the ground curry he mixed each week; it was elegant. I have never since smelled such curry, wonderfully blended with dried orange peel, ginger, chilies, mysterious spices and of course the garlic.

I returned often to buy some and to beg for a few cloves of garlic. In this Indian shop in a remote section of Ndola, I found exotic batiks from Java and West Africa. The shops in town held only cottons imported from Europe; they were pale and uninspired. Zambian women preferred the batiks, and tied them around their waist over a simple cotton dress. This could be pulled off and held over their head in a sudden downpour of rain. These materials were a great discovery but it was garlic that made this shop important to me.

There in the Safeway after being out of the country for two years I experienced feelings of shock, and amazement on seeing such bounty. If I had seen Cortez standing in a room with gold piled to his shoulders I couldn't have been in more awe and wonder. I could reach out and take a full green head of lettuce, any one I wanted; they were all beautiful, crisp, fresh and cool to touch.

How could I choose from such perfection? I put a head of lettuce into my basket. Three fat tomatoes. Could I take four? I shouldn't be greedy. I was tired of cabbage, but it was a habit.

In Ndola it was always a matter of finding enough vegetables for the family meals and there was no choice. We simply took whatever was available. Almost always there was cabbage and sweet potatoes. Sometimes I found carrots and onions. Dare I take a whole handful of garlic?

I felt like Rip van Winkle. It was like waking up and seeing for the first time the stacks and stacks of abundance, the wealth of vegetables and fruit that were piled casually all around. How easy it is to get lost in a memory where food is concerned.

Stories from the Family

Patrick, David, Alice, Chris, Donald in our school uniforms

There Was A Time When ...

John Christian Grube

There was a time when ...

We were on our way to the Dag Hammarskjold Memorial and I was upset and crying as we crossed huge mud puddles in the Peugeot. I'm pretty sure Don was making me worried with his comments on the road conditions being very uncertain. So many monkeys passed by when we stopped the car. We were getting close, or were already inside the boundary of some game reserve, Kafue? I don't know the name. Maybe that's it.

There was a time when ...

It was the first day at some new kindergarten or day care. The setting amazed me. Something about the plush vegetation and rural location helped me to feel comfortable in a very foreign environment.

There was a time when ...

We (my older brothers and dad and my sister, Alice) used to roll old tires around the yard. I might have been just observing the action being that I was kind of short/small, just a little kid. It was like a roller derby with just tires. Very fun though. Wheelbarrows were allowed. Especially if someone was riding in it; probably me. I think I have pictures of this. It was like an early more innocent kinder/gentler version of back yard road warriors.

There was a time when ...

The family used to visit a recreation area; I think it was called Rodwin's lake. Maybe. The premier fun feature was a zip line that traveled across the lake. It was probably just a pond but to me, at the time, it seemed much larger. I was too young to ride. As I watched the older kids and some locals soar above the water and eventually let go and splash down out in the middle somewhere, I thought, I can't wait till I am older.

Over across the lake near some maintenance shack we noticed a commotion. A couple of the employees of the facility were trying to deal with an intruder. Eventually, they pulled out a good sized Boa Constrictor or some large snake that had managed to find a comfortable temporary home inside or underneath a water pump. This was about the size of a riding lawnmower. Well, they were having a heck of a time trying to flush it out of there.

Dag Hammarskjold Memorial Ndola, Zambia

A Sunday Afternoon Drive

Donald Grube

Despite the arguing, we got the windows up in time to save us from that red, brown dust that can clog your nostrils for weeks, or at least most of us survived. Chris was sneezing. That'll teach him to get the window up faster.

It was five minutes of hell every time we passed a truck or car. To avoid choking, it was mandatory to get the windows up before the automobile passed us. Both cars had to slow down and sneak by each other, avoiding the drainage ditches on both sides. Then the drivers had to trudge through the other car's dust for about four minutes, until the fog had lifted. Even rolling up the windows didn't keep the dust from coming in; we still had to tape the hatch back shut and stuff towels in the door jams.

Then, Alice, my older sister, screamed, "There's a snake in the road."

"Oh, Les." My mom said to my father while she grabbed her seat belt. "Slow down! There's a snake in the road."

"Ooh, boss!" said Chris, my younger brother.

"God, that sucker's big," I said, "Hey, Dad, what kind is it?"

My dad's eyes opened wide, turned glassy, and got that look resembling those times when he used to spank us.

"Go around it," my mom said. "Don't run over it. Oh, Les! It may come up from the bottom."

Meanwhile an African lady, with her baby strapped to her

back with a piece of Java print, had already anticipated the danger and had picked up a large stick out of the ditch. My father was just about to squash the six-foot snake–Ba-bump!

"It's dead," he said as he pulled over.

The lady, with the eucalyptus branch in her right hand, began thumping the still very much alive snake. It was crawling awkwardly for shelter in the gutter. Then the baby began to cry. A short cry, then a long silence while it breathed. Then another series, always accompanied by the haphazard beat of the club. Then a young African man rode up on his bicycle and saw that it was his job to kill the already mutilated snake. He ran over to the lady, shouting at the top of his register, grabbed the stick and started pounding the snake into the ground, giving one loud cry for each hit.

The big bloody mess didn't even resemble a snake any more. The lady, sick to her stomach, began throwing up. Gobs of muck came spewing out of her mouth and splashed to the ground.

"Start the car, Les." My mom said.

"Wait a minute," I said. "Mom, I feel sick; let me out."

On top of Ndola Hill

Ndola Nutrition Walk

Singing in the Choir

Alice Hughes

Mom asked me to write a story, a remembrance really, about our time in Zambia. I pondered this request for several months, unable to decide what event or memory to write about. I could write about our arrival in Lusaka and waking up one morning to discover a family of geckos living on the ceiling of my hotel room. Or about the flying ants – they completely grossed me out, especially when one arrived plastered to my chicken one night in the hotel dining room. Or experiencing our first rainstorm and watching the ditches at the side of the road become rushing waterways. Or when it could be raining heavily in the front yard, but be dry as a bone in the backyard. But those remembrances weren't enough for a full story.

What about my days in the convent school? Of needing to wear a uniform, that had a very precise hem length. "It must be no more than four inches off the ground when kneeling." This was, after all, the early seventies, when hem lengths were ridiculously short. The nuns had their limits! Or what about arguing over the spelling of a particular word with Sr. Mary – I don't actually remember which one. She said it was "wrong," when I knew I had learned to spell it that way at school in "America." I also remember thinking how funny it was when someone would ask, "You are from America? Do you know my cousin's best friend's brother who lives in Chicago?" I would then explain that the United States was a

rather large country and California was actually thousands of miles away from Chicago. Or I could write that while in Form 1A, which is like our 7th grade, I discovered that if I wore nail polish I would stop biting my nails. (Folks who know me now, know that I always have perfectly manicured nails. Now you know where that started.)

Then there was my friendship with Fiona. I spent huge amount of time with her and with her family. Her parents were both teachers from England working in the local schools, in much the same way my dad was working with the farmers. Teaching. There was the exciting time she had a bushbaby as a pet. Playing with that nocturnal creature was so much fun. But really, deep inside I was glad and relieved when it was decided that bushbabies shouldn't be pets and she was released properly back to her natural habitat. Learning how to remove ticks from their two dogs ears, now that was an adventure. They were wonderful, beautiful dogs: one a dalmatian, the other an Irish setter. Whatever Fiona did, I did. We would walk home from school each day for dinner (which was really lunch, but that is another story). She was quite tall, so I typically took two steps for each one of her strides. If any of you have ever wondered why I walk the way I do, blame Fiona. I joined the Girls' Brigade, much like Girl Scouts, because Fiona did. I wore the uniform. I loved the cool hat. I still have it tucked away in one of my trunks.

One day Fiona was going to choir rehearsal, so I went too. Frances was the director. She was young and quite beautiful with long brunette hair swept up into a gorgeous ponytail. The choir was all children, although Fiona and I were among the oldest. I loved going to choir rehearsal. I loved singing.

Once we were working on a play, of sorts. It was based on the tunes from Schumann's *Album for the Young*. Lyrics had been added to each the songs and there was some dialogue added to link the songs together and create a story line. There was the soldier, the peasant, the farmer, the orphan, etc. Oh, how I loved these short pieces. I have always had a fondness for those melodies, even when Frances first introduced it I recognized the tunes and where they had originated. Back in San Jose, my friend Megan (daughter of the once mayor of San Jose, Janet Grey Hayes) and I did a pantomime to "The Wild Rider." It was for a performance with her sister playing the piano. I have searched high and low for years to find the publisher of this "musical play" to perform with various children's choirs I have worked with, but much to my dismay I have never been able to locate it in published form. Later in college I worked though Schumann's entire Album with my piano teacher. These gems remain some of my favorites.

The Sound of Music. I believe I did this with the children's choir, or it might have been with the theater company – in any case it was still Frances at the helm. I don't recall it being a full production, but I do recall the rehearsal process. I was to be Luisa, because of my age and height, which meant I needed to sing the lyric "I flit, I float, I fleetly flee, I fly". Well here was a problem. I had quirky way of pronouncing the letter "L," it kind of gurgled in my throat. I had a speech therapist in elementary school try to fix it with such wonderful tongue-twisters as "Lucy loves licking lovely lemon and lime flavored lollies with her lovely lettuce!" Well, it was a struggle. At one point it was suggested that I replace the "L" in each word with an "R". I tried it once but refused to do it this way, as it sounded even more ridiculous. In the end I gurgled my way through the lyric. Later in college, my voice teacher taught me how flip the letter "L" with my tongue. I was so thankful to finally know how to fix it! Occasionally though, I catch myself gurgling an "L" every now and again. I wonder how my niece, the Speech and Language Pathologist, would help someone fix that now?

But the most extravagant production, by far, was "Noyes Fludde" by Benjamin Britten. This is, no doubt, at the foundation of my life-long love of this composer's work. We had a cast of what seemed like thousands. Adults came in to play the adult roles. Fiona and I and some of other older girls were "The Gossips." I loved singing the laughing song. I have never seen the score since, but I can still sing that tune. Then there were also dozens of children who played various animals. I remember helping to make the wonderful masks that they wore. It was performed with great pomp and circumstance in the Anglican Church in Ndola. It was only later, that I found out that there is a wonderful tradition of performances of this in churches in England.

Was singing in the choir the most exciting thing I did when I lived in Zambia? Probably not. My wild escapade with a rhinoceros and the game park ranger pushing me up a tree to safety would fall into that category. My brothers having a monkey as a pet was pretty exciting. Learning the circle of life and watching my dad kill our chickens and ducks for our dinner was an experience worth remembering. There were so many other colorful and delightful memories, but I can't help but think that my experiences with Frances, Schumann and Britten helped shape my current life, in ways that run deeply to my core and to my formation as a musician, singer, conductor, teacher and performer.

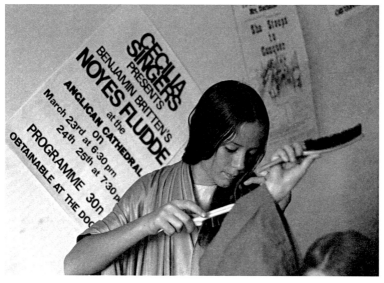

Alice's friend Fiona in front of the poster for Noyes Fludde

Donald, Alice, and Chris with our chicks in the back yard

The Zambian Ministry of Education

David Grube

The hardest part of writing a story about Africa is picking one. We saw so many wonderfuland fabulous places, met so many interesting people and observed them doing unbelievable things. We stayed in several countries in Europe and Africa while traveling to Zambia.

Towards the end of our stay in Ndola four school friends and I traveled halfway across Africa, in a VW bus, to the port city of Dar es Salaam on the Indian Ocean and then up the coast to mombossa and then back to Ndola. That long road trip deserves a story of its own. But I can only pick one story and the one I picked made quite an impact on me at the time and maybe even a little still today.

In 1970, I found out my family was to move to Africa for a couple of years. While waiting for all the preparations to be made, my imagination had already taken off. It was fueled by Hollywood's version of Africa, movies like Tarzan and Abbot and Costello. I searched through a large collection of National Geographic magazines for every picture or article on the subject. I found out that I was going to be traveling to the dark continent on the other side of the hemisphere below the equator.

We all went to the doctors to get shots for typhoid, yellow fever, bilharzia and other diseases that I've never heard of.

Then we all had our passport photos taken. I watched and helped my dad pack a large shipping trunk with a variety of items like recording and photographic equipment, rolls of 35mm, an 8 mm camera, film books and stuff for poultry, lots of fishing gear and a brand-new top-of-the-line shortwave radio. He explained to me that this was to be shipped by sea and would be there sometime before or after our arrival. I knew I was on the edge of a incredible adventure.

Shortly after our arrival at Lusaka, the capital city of Zambia, we moved to Ndola into our first house. There I soon found out that I wouldn't be running through the jungle right away instead I was to be enrolled in school. The name of the school was Kansenji Secondary. In the local Bantu language Chibimba. Kansenji means 'cane rat'. This is a very large rodent from that area with an average body length of about a half of a meter. I thought this to be a strange name for a school. I attended eight classes a day including French, English, algebra, literature, geography, civics, history and art. This was a more intense education than what I was accustomed to back in the States.

I was the only white student in any of my classes. But they classified me as a European, this was something I lightly protested at first; I insisted I was a American; not a European. School was very structured, efficient, and strict. It was based on the Cambridge school system that had been tweaked and changed just enough to fit into a third world country. The Ministry of Education took the business of educating as much of the population of Zambia as possible very seriously. The first rule of every day was punctuality, respect and tidiness. I remember standing in a large hallway with five other students. We were all dressed the same. Short pants, black leather shoes, knee socks and a button down shirt with a tie. They all probably had better excuses than me for being tardy. Two of them were my friends, and I knew they lived more than 5 km away in one of the townships surrounding Ndola. They would walk to school barefoot and then before entering school grounds they would take their kneesocks and shiny shoes out of their book bags and put them on.

I have been in this hallway almost a handful of times by now, mostly for being tardy and once for being bringing fireworks to school. The first time I was here, after waiting, I finally entered the deputy headmasters office. He scolded me for being late and told me that I probably thought the punishment here was uncivilized. Then he said that I was lucky because in America they shoot students. He then laid an old copy of the times of Zambia newspaper on the desk in front of me. The front page read, "four students shot and killed at Kent State University in the United States." And then after that I received my first three strikes with a bamboo cane.

One time on my way to school after being distracted and losing track of time, I knew I was late, so I decided to cut school altogether. I took off my tie and stashed my book bag and started off towards the marketplaces. I was almost there when all of a sudden there was a loud ringing bell behind me. It was a cop ringing the bell on his bicycle. His uniform consisted of short pants, kneesocks, black shoes, a shiny belt with a small billy club and a large set of antique handcuffs hanging from them and a whistle hanging from his shirt. He said, "You young boy, why are you not in school?" I told him that my classes have been canceled. He said, "Where are you from?" When I told him America, he got all the way off his bicycle and told me that I must tell him all about America.

I told him that the people in America, only worked eight hours a day, five days a week and after that they were paid overtime, and that most people owned their own houses and had two cars. And that the policemen all drove cars or motorcycles, and had 38 or 357 pistols on their belts, but they had cheap shiny handcuffs not like the strong sturdy ones that he had.

He told me about the village he had grown up in, and that because of the colonial rule he didn't have the opportunity to go to school. His only way out of the village was to join Zambian army or the police force. I finally fessed up to him and told him why I was not in school and that it was too nice a day to be caned.

He told me the punishment seem fair to him and that I should not avoid it. I told him I would not avoid it again, but couldn't promise him that I wouldn't be tardy in the future. He became my friend and I met and talked to him several times after that. Just before returning to the states I had finally talked him into selling me his handcuffs. They were important to him for his job and he also used them to lock his bicycle. He told me that he had found another pair of handcuffs. We then agreed on a price of five kwacha which is about seven US dollars.

When I returned to America, the next school I went to was Santa Cruz High School. I had seen and learned a lot in Africa. I still have that pair of handcuffs in my collection of souvenirs from Africa.

My Trip to Africa

Tim Donatelli

Tim is David's friend who came for a visit.

I was about 16 years old when I was invited to visit my friend David and family. I had not been on a plane before. I left San Francisco and flew to New York, then to Belgium. I remember this because I had a long layover. I was exhausted. I found a lounge for moms and kids where I asked the attendant what I should do. She said they would wake me for my flight on time to fly to Athens. I remember this because the airport is on the water. I thought for sure we were going to land in the water. The next flight was to Lusaka the capital of Zambia. Then I missed my flight to Ndola, because I could not understand the call. Les called the airport to find where I was, then I caught the next flight.

First thing I noticed was left hand drive. Not good for a young driver. First couple of days was getting used to a different place. David and I went with Les (who I thought was a great guy). We went to a village to see what he did. There was a lake that reminded me of Crater Lake in Oregon. We watched boys dive in the lake. They asked if we would like to try. No way. They were diving from way up high. We went to other villages for his work. I could not believe the way people lived.

David and I and some of his friends went out one night driving around town. I had never before seen a *round-a-bout*. I kept wanting to drive on the right side of the road. There

was one girl that I fell in love with and now I wonder what happened to her.

One trip we took was to a Game Park. On the drive there we were on gravel roads with trucks all over the place. We went across the big bridge and armed soldiers were everywhere. They pulled us over and told us to drive 25 mph. Apparently Les did not drive that slowly; half way across the bridge a guard stepped onto the roadway with his gun. Les stopped the car; the guard came around to the driver side with his gun still pointed at the car and asked what speed we were doing. Then he reminded us to slow down. I almost pooped my pants. When we arrived at the game park we were the only group there. There was a war going on somewhere close I guess. It was cool. Dave and I had our own little hut. An armed guard took us for hikes.

One time Dave and I asked the head guy about some weed. After convincing him we would not turn him in he told us to go to a little village. We sat in some chairs that were so cool. (I wish I had a drawing of one). The guy was very interested in the way we lived in the USA. It was fun talking to him. He had this other guy go to a different village to get weed. The guy had a loincloth on and no shoes. He took off like a rocket. He came back about twenty minutes later. We went back to our little hut and had a smoke. I still have never had any that was that good.

Later Les came to the door and said "How about a walk?" (Oh, why not? We are ripped.) We started off along a creek. There were a lot of birds and giraffes. We were on a trail where an elephant had done his business. The guard stepped over, Les stepped over, I stepped over, David hit it dead center. I was laughing so hard I almost fell down. (Oh, by the way, the guard who was in full uniform at this time was the guy who ran off to get the grass for us). We went further down the path and then circled back. We came around a bunch of brush and the guard got all excited and told us to get in this tree. After climbing it, he points to a rhino down a ways and the rhino is not happy. He apparently got a whiff of us and was pawing the ground and throwing his head around. I remember his big old horn. He eventually lost interest and then we went back to the camp. The rest of the stay was uneventful.

David and I flew home together. We went to Rome. It was fantastic. We walked everywhere; saw some great stuff. Last thing about the trip we bought switchblades in Rome (cool). We flew into San Francisco. We were a little nervous; I had probably five or six knifes in my pockets. Customs did not say a word. Try that today. This is my story.

Found In The Jungle

PJ Grube

You don't have to be David Livingstone to be lost in a jungle or to discover an amazing place like deepest darkest Africa. For each of us, finding the unknown wild requires little more than stepping out our backdoor. In this story, my backdoor just happens to be Livingstone's jungle in Africa.

Discovering the unknown takes action. For some, fear leads to fear, leads to inaction. For others opening up to life anew leads to the wonders of the next amazing thing. As children we open to a world with all our senses. We figure and calculate what is. We let the unknown into our bodies, minds and our spirit, to participate, comprehend, and share the experience. We dream, put dreams into action and the dream becomes fruit. Love of life, truth to amazement, or fear becomes our fantasy guide to disaster. "Why are we in the jungle?" is not the question; however, "in the jungle" is the answer.

I am number three of seven kids. Mom and Dad brought five of us on their African journey; my older siblings, Steve and Anne, came later to visit. They stayed behind, in the States, to attend college plus Steve was in the Army Reserves.

I don't really know why Mom and Dad decided to go to Africa. One would think it was an opportunity to experience an unknown land or, given their skills, a desire to share their knowledge and experience with others.

However, looking back, it might really have been a chance

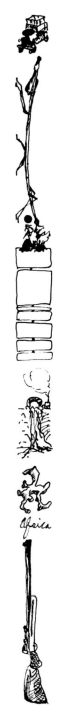

for the family to escape the turbulence of our times. In the 60's and 70's the United States was rolling with war protests, social and political turmoil, riots and even assassinations. People were demanding their rights and people were being shot down.

But whatever the reason, "What better place than Africa for discovery, opportunity and escape?" The continent was leaving its colonial past behind and the people were building new governments and communities.

Mom and Dad sent out employment applications to a bunch of developing nations and were offered a position by the newly independent government of Zambia. Dad's job was to share his valuable knowledge of poultry and egg production with the developing communities there. He was made a provisional poultry officer and we were stationed in the little town of Ndola, in the Copper Belt Province.

I went to Kansenji Secondary School and hung-out-n-about with the other teenagers. We were the minority, a hand full of whites in a sea of black faces. The people were welcoming and curious about who we were and where we came from; we were curious of them too. We were well accepted. Most expatriates sent their children to boarding schools. "What's the point of that?"

My brother David and I got to live in the servants' quarters at the back of our government assigned housing. We didn't have servants but most of the expatriates did. Every house in the *Kansenji* District had a servant quarters. This neighborhood was previously called the Queen Victoria District but after independence the newly formed government re-named it Kansenji (it means Cane Rat). The area had been the colonialist' suburb and they had cloistered themselves there like rats in a thicket of bamboo cane.

One summer Steve and Anne came to visit. Steve was on vacation and Anne was on her own journey. After visiting with us for a couple of weeks she was going off to an ashram in India to study with a famous yogi.

The four of us older kids, Steve, Anne, David, and myself decided to see the wonders of Zambia. We loaded up the Peugeot wagon and drove south to Victoria Falls and the giant Kafue Game Reserve. That's where our story begins, where Livingston's ended, to discover the next bright light in the darkness of our unknown.

The highway south cuts through the dense Miombo Woodland, a plateau of tropical and sub-tropical savanna. It is only a small part of a vast floodplain and massive ecosystem that spreads out through the heart of Africa. It has an amazing variety of wildlife, including many large herds of big game mammals.

Feeding this varied and abundant life is the Zambezi River and its several tributaries. It is the fourth longest river in Africa and flows fifteen hundred ninety nine miles south through seven thirsty countries. From the headwaters at Kalene Hill on the Zambian/Congolese border in the north, it collects waters south through Angola. West of the Kafue Game Reserve it increases strength through its tributaries on the plateau of the western interior of Zambia. As it shifts east it snakes along the Namibia panhandle, touching the very tip of Botswana, and moves along the Zambia/Zimbabwe border, where Victoria Falls is located. The river continues to Lake Kariba the world's largest man made lake, then to Lake

Cabora Bassa, in Mozambique, Africa's fourth largest artificial lake, before the river finally flows into the Indian Ocean.

The highway south was a two-lane-wide dirt-gravel road with a single lane of asphalt paved down the middle. When there is an approaching car each vehicle moves half-off the tarmac, with the right two wheels on the pavement and left two wheels on the gravel. That's right we drive on the left-hand side of the road and the gigantic mining lorries don't move off the pavement – "Get out of the way!"

As in any lengthy car ride various conversations abound. Each mile traveled away from home brought to mind tales and legends we'd heard through our young lives. Now, the truth or fiction of these stories was before us.

Many fears fell away with each new sighting of the awesome and amazing. But there's 'reason for caution' in the untamed world. Susceptibility to diseases like malaria, bilharzia, sleeping sickness, and dysentery are real and ever present in the African interior. But the many stories so widely propagated by the media and movies became myth when we witnessed the thriving grass-hut villages and gardens stretching through 'The Bush'. We saw colorful native attire, beautiful headdresses, drummers and wild dancers. All these made ridiculous the commercialized idea of the angry native spearman; radical nose piercing, and hungry cannibals with their boiling pots.

By inquiry, we actually met a witch doctor, the thought of which would have normally scared us to death; shaking ritual rattles; sacred powders cast into the air; and our purified spirits offered up to the village chieftain. However, our minds were spared these horrifying scenarios. In reality he was a very kind man, casually dressed in khakis and a collared work shirt. He invited us into his hut. We bowed under a low archway, and accepted, graciously, a grip of hand-rolled herbal smokes in exchange for a lift into a neighboring village. Herbal smoke filled the thatched mud hut.

The spell of a witch doctor's herbs is as real as a dream of an unknown place the description of which defies words. We soon found ourselves letting the doctor out of the car at a Chibuku stand in a village a mile down the road.

Chibuku is a maize beer – brewed from the last, of last year's maize crop. Maize, what Americans know as corn, is stored in bamboo silos and the last of it gets a little, well... Chibuku is a milky refreshing beer like drink and fairly intoxicating, as we found out.

On we go. It was a curious feeling the first time I saw a bulbous Baobab tree, storing water for the dry season, or the tall umbrella trees, the top leafs and branches well out of reach of towering giraffes. Impressive are the twenty-foot anthills. I knelt down in wonder to see ceaseless lines of marching ants, building stone by stone a towering castle. The multitude entombed an entire tree as the bones for their home; and the tree lives.

At the Zimbabwe border the Zambezi river opens to the widest sheet of falling water in the world, the Mosi-oa-Tunya waterfall ("smoke that thunders"), which Livingstone renamed Victoria Falls.

It is impressive. The ever-moving waters of the Zambezi pulse through a land filled with life. The mile-and-a-quarter wide rift in the plateau suddenly swallows this enormous flow in an abyss with a thunderous crash, pounding out voluminous clouds of moisture from the crevasse. The waters rage through a narrow channel creating a deafening sound. It's roils roll fifty-feet high in what is called "The Boiling Pot".

We followed a trail down into an overgrown rainforest; down through the earth' canyon-crack as cascading rain pelted the giant foliage above our heads. The violent river seemed to tower over our heads, held back only by the shear cliffs of the mighty canyon walls. There is a momentary blindness when one witnesses such beauty, like after look-ing into a light; it takes a moment for sight to re-adjust. The blazed image on the retina holds it's own images a while lon-ger. I was profoundly shaken by the beating arterial rhythms of this eternal flow and I sensed I was inside the body of God…

Having reached our southern destination we decided to take a more *circuitous* route back north into the Kafue Game Reserve, a path through the wild western interior. We drove into the jungle.

The opening was a tarmac road, which led to a gravel road and as we traveled it soon turned into tire tracks, and then it was just tall, tall grass everywhere. The trail was gone. The four of us, our little Peugeot wagon, and our witch doc-tor herbs were well into the jungle somewhere in deepest darkest Africa. We had no clue as to which way to go.

These are the times that knowing who you are is the answer to being lost and finding who you are is the real challenge. A grain of sand in your pocket might be the only touchstone back to the moment.

"So where are we?"

"We are here, and 'this is paradise.'"

"Find the road! Look at the map!"

"There's just the one. There aren't any roads! It's just one big block of green."

"Are there any rivers or streams?"

"Yeah. Which one? Which is which? We have no reference points or signs."

"There aren't any features?"

"Look! Even a topography map wouldn't help us. Its a giant plateau… a floodplain."

"Ok. Where do we go? Forward or backward?"

"If we drive north we're sure to find a road."

"Isn't that what Livingston said, 'I am prepared to go anywhere, provided it be forward.'"

We agreed. We kept moving forward. As we drove we slowly emerged from the thick jungle foliage. Having left so-called civilization behind, I had a sense we'd made a good choice. It seemed a time past had became a time present, and we were traveling through a pre-history land of bounty and plenty. For a long while there was no trace of any human activity.

"We're all one in a perfect ecosphere." I thought. There were elephants, slumbering lions, tall giraffes, and millions of blue ball monkeys. At one point we stopped to see an elephant off in the distance. We got out to take a picture and it began to trot towards us.

"Oh look! He wants to come say hi!"

His trot became a snorting gallop, waving his massive tusks.

"He doesn't look happy."

"Quick! Get in the car."

We piled in and started off with the rogue elephant well on our heels. As we sped away, our attention was fixed on the angry elephant. Stephen's eyes were wide in the rearview mirror. A cloud of dust swirled behind as the beast began to slow down and reared up in victory. This was not the circus tent.

This is a large land with swaths of thick forest bush broken by open savanna and grass. Grass so tall you can only see the horizon.

As a more established dirt road appeared we began to see thatched mud-huts and people. We saw slash and burn areas where five acres at a time were being prepared for village gardens. In these areas the land had been striped bare of the woodland leaving only the anthills and smoldering mounds of dirt-covered woodpiles. The pyres were a slow-burn process converting the harvested wood into charcoal fuel for the copper smelters.

Huge mining lorries travel these interior roads. The trucks are notorious for flipping over and their chassis are bent. They seem to have a yaw as they move sideways down the road toward you.

The lorries carry copper ore and collect the charcoal from the villagers. The monies they received for the charcoal help these agrarian communities buy in the city things they cannot grow or make in the village.

Like most things in the country these lorries had multiple uses. On their return trips these massive dump trucks are filled with workers and villagers like a bus.

Everyone stepped to the side as these giant beasts roared past with powerful entitlement. As the roar subsided and the dust cloud settled, the waffled roads left little doubt that life in the bush was changing. After all it was the mines that built the roads with revenue from resource-hungry foreign capitalists. My awful thought was, "On the road of independence, these small communities produce a charcoal byproduct that would heat the crucible of a ferocious, consuming market place, striping their country of its mineral wealth, and plow under their agrarian paradise."

Here in Africa, natural interruptions on a summer day are momentary torrential downpours of life giving rain. One moment blue sky, and the next, thick black clouds drench the countryside with raindrops the size of your thumb. The villagers were unflustered by these occurrences and would gather under the nearest tree. They seemed to be sharing the day's weight with each other while waiting for the next blue sky. The clouds would part and everyone went on about their day.

The parched porous red soil guzzled the rain like a sieve. Everything was brighter, fresher, and greener as the earth poured forth a fountain of green foliage with exploding victorious blossoms rallying to the delight of being. There is no mistaking the life of this world. The trees breathe, and the choirs of birds announce the bounty around them. They fill the trees and then the sky in waves of rolling anthems settling to feast and then flash in flight again. The world here drinks in everything, all of a sudden, and bit by bit, together in marvelous symmetry. The whole of life at its brightest and each piece brighter because of it. This is defiantly the garden from whence all life sprung, each beautiful thing, together, whole in its nature.

And so we traveled, and it was like that, until the washboard roads, corrugated by the mining lorries and heavy torrents of rain, became more common and the jungle paradise gave way to the subdued open road, and a rail line led north. We were back on the tarmac road to Ndola.

I don't know what of it was a dream, but now, it's all a dream. It all had a life of it's own; the stories of the adventure replace the experience; a time past remains the past; and today is its own day. What we found we could not have known and what we found became our own. We saw it, felt it, and claimed it for that moment. A dream, then an experience, and it's a dream again.

I will never look at our world as anything less than an amazing miraculous garden again. Today it is off to the next unknown in the garden of bounty and plenty. I must open, and take it in.

PJ Grube looking back forty-five years

Twenty-foot high ant hill, built bit by bit by ceaseless lines of marching ants, the multitude entombing an entire living tree as a design for their towering castle and the tree lives.

We witnessed the thriving grass-hut villages and gardens stretching into *the bush*.

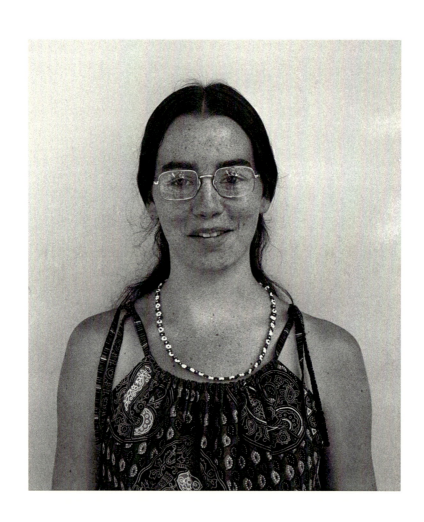

Anne's Story

Not long ago PJ was having breakfast with Anne and they talked about when she came to Zambia to visit the rest of the family, Anne remembered, "Steve and I went together on the plane. We went to Amsterdam and England, but we ended up in Africa where I spent about a month. England was nice. You expect the Beatles to pop out everywhere. Paul, George, John and Ringo."

"What do you remember most about Africa?"

Anne thought for a minute and responded, "The trees are fantastic. Everything was different from San Jose or Santa Cruz. The people, dark brown, black and the women wore beautiful colored dresses. Yeah, that was cool. The people seemed real nice you know."

All was quiet for a few minutes and then she said, "On the way home, I went to India."

Quotes from letters from India:

September, 1971

Dear Mom and Dad,

A lot has happened since I saw you last. Kerry and I just got back yesterday from Mangalore. We had a wonderful week of swimming in the Arabian Sea. It's beautiful, clean, warm; no one else goes there except every Sunday night to watch the sunset. They come and go within a couple of hours. It's really a site – all the beautiful sari's and other things you see.

In Mangalore I bought myself two sari's. The blouses and skirt (slip) are being made and will be sent in a couple of days. I've already learned how to wrap one – not as difficult as I thought.

Today, Vincent (the cook) taught me to wash clothes on a rock. I have lots to keep me busy – learning to cook rice, reading, music, visiting the missionaries (a man and a woman). I can do some baking in their oven.

Last night I saw my first rain – very heavy.

Well, keep in touch. Don't worry. Love, Anne"

October 10, 1971

"I have been at the Ashram now since the 6th. I know I will be learning much in one month. If things work out well here, I would like to stay the three months. I will be learning much more here about life and living than I could possible learn at a University. It's a big chance for me. It will be of great use to me and others. I really want to stay for a while. Hope that you see the worthwhileness of my staying . Looking forward to hearing from you. Peace, Anne"

October 25, 1971

"The monsoons have come to Pondecherry. The last five days it has been raining constantly. This first month at the Ashram is almost over and I'd like to stay for the next two months which will be the completion of the first half of his 6 month course. There is much to learn and I'm very eager to learn it."

December 1971

"I was sad to leave the Ashram and all my friends, especially Swami Gitamanda. I have a certificate and a note of recommendation from Swami to teach Yoga when I so desire. There is a lot I wish I could tell you about what I have learned but it's really impossible in a letter. Part of it is understanding or getting a new perspective of where we fit into this whole Universe."

January 1, 1972

"Happy New Year! It seems as if I've been away from the States for years. Strange. Well, not too much more to say but I'm fine, hope the family is ok. I feel both happy and sad about returning. One thing nice about returning is that there aren't really any loose ends to tie up. I'll mostly just be starting off on my own, finally. It's a good feeling but also brings with it a tinge of fearfulness. I feel now I can say that I'm more equipped to handle things. But there's so much more to learn. I miss you all. Lots of love, Anne"

January 6, 1972

"Hello! On the plane now from Tokyo to Honolulu and then to San Francisco. Everything has gone quite well. Overnight in Calcutta and Tokyo was pleasant. Glad to get a warm bath and some sleep there. Hope things are ok where you are. Will mail this when I get to San Francisco. Goodbye for now, Anne"

Chickens in Africa

Stephen Grube

I'll start fifteen years after the Grube family returned from Africa. I was working in a large engineering company near Santa Cruz. One day an engineer friend of mine who already knew that my family had lived in Africa, walked up and said, "Hey Steve, you have to meet my friend Bruce who just joined the company." So Jim and I called Bruce over and after introductions Jim said, "Steve's family actually went to Africa to raise chickens!"

The funny part of this is, that a few years earlier, when they were renting and sharing a house in Santa Cruz, they had an expression they used once in a while when something was looking unlikely or had some huge barrier to completion. You might hear: "Yeah, like raising chickens in Africa." Well, from their university studies they were familiar with E. F. Schumacher, *Small is Beautiful,* and the concept of "appropriate technology." For them the phrase referred to an "ideal" – the chance to actually work at the grassroots level and affect many people's lives with tools and skills for a lifetime.

My parents were doers. In 1970 my family moved to Zambia, Africa for about two and a half years. The well-considered plan was that my father would work in the various rural remote villages and teach African households and communities how to raise chickens, which included participating in the local economy. (You may read more about this

in the other stories in this book.)

They contracted directly with the Zambian government rather than tying-up with one of the various NGOs or organizations such as USAID. They had already understood from their work in the fifties and sixties in the social justice and civil rights movements in Santa Clara Valley, that the community dynamic – involving purpose, commitment and broad participation – was powerful for effecting meaningful change.

It's interesting to see how we affect the lives of others – often in unexpected ways – and it's easy to underestimate our effect on others. What would we find if we visited Ndola, Zambia again – now, almost fifty years later? If we looked hard would we find someone in business today that was first propelled by Lester Grube, or would we find someone that remembers the Grube family in some special, life-long way? Almost certainly there are ripple effects from the energy and knowledge we brought with us at the time. It's pleasant to think about.

Lester's Africa

This text is from a cassette audio-recording made by the Lester Grube family in Zambia, 1971, transcribed by his son PJ Grube. "This excerpt, in his own words describes his work and observations after three months on the job; however, what could not be transcribed is the loving, compassionate and humanitarian voice of my father."

My Little Flock of Chicks

Well I can't resist telling you about my little flock of chickens. They are really doing well. The last six days I have 19 pullets; I've had two days of 19 eggs and four days of 18 eggs, which is about 96 1/2% average, and we're doing it on something less than, right around a quarter of a pound of feed per day. Actually the chicken pen is like Grand Central Station; the kids are going in and out all day and they sit in there and think and pet the chickens, and the little guys go in and out and collect the eggs, and I go in and out and collect the eggs. We're checking them at all hours, which is kind of contrary for what you are supposed to be doing with chickens. With layers you reduce their efficiency if you keep bothering them all the time. These birds are something else.

We've got one feeder made out of a six-foot piece of the biggest bamboo we could find in our backyard (4" diameter) and we just cut a trough out of it, but that is a little bit too shallow, so I always put about a pound and a half of the 4 1/2 to 5 pounds a day in that and the rest I put in a four gallon vegetable oil tin which I've cut and hung from a tripod. The

birds can't get into it. It's a common thing they use in the rural areas around here for feeders and it works out pretty well. Incidental to that I've got a line on an opportunity to get a lot of these cans to be used by our bush farmers. I got them for nothing. The oil company that handles this stuff, apparently gets a lot of damaged tins coming in and they have to pour the oil out of them and put it into other things, other tins or bottles I guess. They just give them away and I picked up 146 last Friday, and each one can be used as a feeder for about 15 chickens. Anyway, the farmers get them for nothing and cut them themselves and hang them from the rafters in their rural poultry houses, so it works pretty well. They also use the darn things for their water, and can use them for nests too, so they really are making use of everything.

Our Involvement

As long as I'm talking about poultry I will explain to you what our main involvement is in the poultry section. Actually, the work here is split up into commercial farmers, cooperatives, the rural poultry scheme and women's clubs. The only ones that we have money available to do any development work for is the women's clubs and the rural poultry scheme. So that's where most of our staff is concentrated and where most of our time is concentrated. Incidentally it's probably the most single successful development program in Zambia whether its agriculture or whatever it is, since 1965, when the first loans were given to the first farmers. When they started there were only 800 birds in the hands of Zambian farmers. Since then, as of 1971, we have 50,000 birds in the hands of rural farmers scattered all over Zambia. The way this works is: the project. They build an agricultural camp in the area and this camp has an agricultural assistant who's there. Then they build a development project around that camp and the farmers within 5 - 6 miles use that as a kind of training center, ultimately. They have one poultry unit there, as a demonstration project and put a kitchen there for the use of the farmers. But this scheme was successful I think because it was a well laid out program and each step along the way the farmers are given training as a group. After each step, they go out and do that step on their own. For instance house building – they learn to do this. They work on the building of a house in this agricultural camp. Then they go back and make bricks for their own out of anthill mud and they build their house according to our specifications. And then the next step of house building is done as a demon-stration project and then they go back and do that. Then, they learn to brood the chicks and then they go back and do that. And each one of these is followed up by our staff to see that they're doing it correctly in the project. So it has two things about it; it has the training, which is very thorough, and then the follow-up by our staff; and we have about 16 staff out in the field in the rural areas doing this work in the Copperbelt Province, which incidentally is about 120 by 120 miles square.

So they get a government loan, for roughly 400 kwacha, which is stateside about $560. This includes buying the pul-lets, furnishing the equipment and feed to get the birds to peek production, which they figure would be eight months of age; two months into the production. And then they have to start paying the loan back and start saving money to buy replacements and to buy their own feed for cash. Well this is the way the program works. Well, some of them of course fail, but over 50% of them have not only paid their loans back but have saved to buy replacement birds and even expand. So it's a very heartening thing. Because this is the first money that these people have had a chance to handle in the rural areas, and first cash crop they've ever had. And they figure they have one chance to make a success of it. They do this. They're taught some bookkeeping, as well as, not bookkeeping, but financial things they need to know, not as complicated as bookkeeping because many of them can't read or write. They can only speak their own native tongue, which is possibly Bemba, might be Lamba or some other dialect. So that is where most of our money is concentrated, the development money, and where our time and staff is concentrated.

Communal Cooperatives

They used to have communal cooperatives several years ago, shortly after independence, say, where they had a laying house project, laying hen project, with a 1000 birds. Everybody worked on this project communally; they divided up the time and this sort of thing. It turns out that these were not successful because it was kind of contrary to the history of the people here. They were used to working as family units on their own projects and having their own land and this kind of thing. They work cooperatively together, and they may share some ways of their life, but they were independent. Well, this communal thing was contrary to that and ultimately they have, almost all of them, have failed. Out of about eight of them, there are only a couple small ones that are left, and they're not doing very well. Then there's two resettlement schemes which are operated at Kaputa and Kafuba, which is about 30 miles from here and they are dealing with a large number of families, 250 to 280 families in each one of these. They have a lot of central services provided like water, roads, and school buildings, this kind of thing, and then they independently have their own farms where they will raise vegetables, poultry and pigs, and this sort of thing. So, they're producing about 30,000 dozen a month in these two places.

Commercial Farms

There are some Zambians, who are natives here, who are now emerging as commercial farmers on their own. Maybe they've worked in the mines for a while, saved a little money. Now they buy a farm and go into production on their own. Or they have a business in town, and they saved their money and want to get back on the land and go into production. So we have one man on our staff, Mr. Kalawanda, who's a really sharp guy, who handles the commercial farmers and the cooperatives. And then Mr. Muwatsa and Mr. Inuagwai handle the rural poultry scheme and the women's project, and I sort of supervise everything. I spent the first three months here just learning from him what I was suppose to be doing and how everything was working and just now beginning to take over the reins and get a feel.

Production Issues

The cost of production is probably about 26 ngwee a dozen and they're getting about 40 ngwee in the stores. Our main problem has been the erratic feed deliveries. Well, I think we have that taken care of. This nationalized cultural marketing board has agreed to deliver feed to our rural areas to our rural poultry scheme.

The other main problem is marketing. We have a poultry and egg marketing union, which is about three years old now, which everybody had high hopes for. It was going to be the marketing agent for all of Zambia, ultimately, and do broilers and the whole thing. Well it has fallen flat on its face. They've never been able to get a proper marketing man in to run it and they've had all kinds of financial problems, and are now essentially bankrupt but just hanging on while people try to figure out what to do with the organization.

I have some involvement with that. I'm on the management operations committee and the advisory committee, which meets weekly and also meets monthly. Two different committees, but I'm kind of restricted because that's under the wing of the cooperative and I'm here in the civil service, in spite of the fact it is a major problem for the poultry raiser here and that's in the Department of Agriculture. I can't really act as anything accept as an advisor because it's a different department and it's not under the marketing department, so everybody's acting as advisor to the darn thing. It's really messed, so I'm going to have to find some independent distributors to handle it, selling the eggs for the rural farmers. Myself, we have one project, the new project, 60 miles out in the bush from Ndola, which will be in production in two months. They will be producing about 35 cases a week, so I have to find a place for those to go.

Civil Service

Civil service thing is really something new to me. I haven't ever worked in it before. Of course. And all my background is being able to do any kind of thing I wanted in business essentially. Make the decisions on my own. If I was wrong I had to live with it. If I was right that was big. While civil service, everything is so bound up in the chain of command. You can only go through this person to get to the next person. Everybody's jealous of their position and if you go beyond somebody, work around them, then you have real problems. It is something I have to get used to and it slows things down a little bit, and I have to learn how to write the proper kind of letters and make reports all the time, this kind of stuff. But other than that, the work is really interesting and I'm enjoying it very much.

The staff that I work with is really good and I think quite capable. I would hope that some of these people would stay on, and unless they can get a degree like I had they can't get the salary. What happens is most of them leave after a while. Either that or they're stuck in a lower level. We have two people with 20 years or more service, who just have short course training in poultry, a lot of practical experience in the administration of poultry, but then, they're stuck at a level that they're never going to command very much of a salary. So that's a problem of how to overcome this. I've been working on some ideas along this line to get some educational programs going that would maybe coordinate the University here with someplace like Cal Poly or other colleges, agricultural colleges in the States where they could do two years here two or three years there and then get a degree. Then come back and do more practical work and some day be eligible for the kind of post that I'm filling and they could start hiring in the future. So that's pretty much what the poultry thing looks like.

A Pause

There now let me see what else I have to say. Just let me shut this machine off for a second. . . . . Well let's see . . . . . I took a little breather, got myself a glass of sherry and I made some notes and I find that I left out a couple of things you might be wondering about.

Women's Clubs

One of them is, I said something about the women's clubs and never went on to explain exactly what that involved. This, in a sense I guess, started as sort of a political thing. The district governors and the political appointees wanted something that they could get involved in and get women involved in. Anyway the idea sprung up and they have women's clubs in all of the townships and in some of the rural areas now. They do various things like sewing and nutrition, vegetable growing, and they also do poultry. And as I said, some of our development money goes for this work. Unfortunately we haven't, in the past anyway, had the close supervision or the detailed training of the large numbers in the women's clubs. The result has not been too good. As an example, some of the things that happen, they get pullets, they own pullets and they get them up to laying age and sell them all off to the market before they ever lay an egg. But the

difference in this program is this money is a direct out-and-out grant, not a loan. They just tightened up on the program this year when we were at the poultry conference in Lusaka. It was decided that no club would get a second grant. They were allowed only one grant and that was it, period. So the women, maybe one or two of the women, go for training at the Society of Farmer Training Institute. But other than that, the group of them is not trained. Again, this is one of the chief faults, I think, with the program. It is a communal project where they all share the work in the project and somebody is supposed to make sure that the receipts, that the eggs are all sold and handle the money and this kind of thing.

Well, there hasn't been sufficient training, apparently, for the women to know what's involved in working it; to get on as a community project like this. And the result is that they end up having some disagreements. Some of the clubs will shut down. They decide they will just sell their birds and forget it and will go do something else. So there is a problem there, and that's, I guess, one of the things that I'm going to be, hopefully, trying to straighten out in the next couple of years. I hope it doesn't take that long.

The National Plans

They're just completing the first national plan, which is a five-year plan. And I've been going to some meetings on the second national plan and in that are plans for spending something like 80 or 100 thousand kwacha to build a processing plant in Copperbelt Province in the city of Kitwe, because of this need up here. Now whether that will ever come through or not is up for speculation. The other thing is with farmers, all farmers, except Kafubu and Kafulafuta, market their own eggs. Even the rural farmers, find their own markets. They bring their eggs into town once a week and go back with feed. The rural farmers especially have a real problem, because obviously, they don't have money for transportation, except those that have been in since '65 and maybe expanded to two or three or four units, and have found a way to buy a pickup truck of some kind to get in. But most of them, the rural farmers, are on bicycles and 20 miles round-trip or even 20 miles one way, just doesn't seem to faze them. They carry eggs in one way and go out with 100 pounds of feed on the back of the bicycle. It's just fantastic.

The women too, when they go into the rural areas they walk five, ten miles in, with a baby on the back and something on their head and a basket in hand. It's really fantastic. These are some of the things I want to take pictures of; which I haven't done yet. I'll be sending you some of them.

But anyway, that's the situation. The marketing is done by the farmers. And the dangerous thing is, as production continues to expand, we have no organized marketing system in Zambia. So you don't have the opportunity to find, or call somebody in Lusaka, where they might be short of eggs, and we're long on eggs in Ndola, and this sort of thing. I was hoping I'd be able to get involved with setting something like that up. But after talking to my boss in Lusaka, I'm not so sure that that's going to come off because he says that I'm extension, and that is a marketing problem. The marketing department should be doing it and not me. I can act as an advisor in some things but other than that, no.

I guess that just about winds up my little program for the night. Thank you and I hope you didn't all go to sleep.

President Hastings Kamuzu Banda of Malawi and
President Kenneth Kaunda of Zambia on a visit to Ndola.

Through A Rearview Mirror

When we returned from Zambia we settled in Santa Cruz.
I entered UCSC. This was written in one of my classes.

I am trying to remember a few events that happened during the two years we lived in Zambia that would be relevant to attitudes toward older people. McCluhan says we can't really see our own environment until we have passed it and look at it, as through a rear-view mirror. Experience in another culture is a way of getting a different perspective on our own. This is very limited as our way of seeing things clings to us; we can get inside only through the tiny cracks in our cultural shell. In a cross-cultural experience, dis-orientations occur in various degrees depending on the person and the cultures. At worst, persons are completely unable to cope with the anxieties and experience "cultural shock" to such a degree that they are physically ill. At best, our cultural shell is cracked enough to let us get some new impressions, new ideas and broaden our horizons. As my observations are personal, the only perspective I can take is one of how things seemed to me and how I felt; to be more exact, I should say, the only perspective I can take is how I am perceiving them now; that is, through a rear-view mirror, with the distance and the narrow view which that allows.

My first new and personal impression was when I was addressed as "mama". This was by an older man at the airport. I thought it was a comment on the fact that I was holding the hand of my four-year old and several of the other children were clustered close to me. The term made me feel good. My husband was often called "bwana". I thought this had all kinds of undesirable connotations from colonialism. Zambia had been an independent country for only six years when we arrived in 1970. At a tea several British women, who had been in Zambia a long time, said that they preferred to be called "madam"; for them, "mama" meant middle age and they didn't want to think of themselves that old. I liked the term: partly because "Mama" made me think of the universality of motherhood, and the tone and manner in which it was spoken conveyed affection and honor.

Traditionally in Zambia, honor is greater as persons grow older. Even after the colonial experience, migration to find work in the copper mines, and the adjustment to the continuing technological and economic changes of a developing country; the attitudes of a matrilineal society are still present among the Bemba people of north and northeastern Zambia. President Kaunda came from Malawi and grew up among the Bemba. His mother is a part of his household and given a place of honor on state occasions. I remember reading in the newspaper an interview with him about his mother. He told why he felt it was important to listen to her advice and how young people should honor the old traditional ways, as taught by their elders.

We attended a village agricultural fair, where Les, my husband, had been working with poultry farmers. I was watching from behind the crowd as a man played a drum and a woman sang. An older man, who seemed to have some authority saw my interest, and maneuvered me into a front position. I was touched with his concern for me and felt that he thought the performance was important. There was singing and everyone was caught up in the rhythm of the drums; then I realized what it was about. The song was in Cibemba, so my whole understanding came from the mood and the gestures and the intensity and emotional response of the audience. She was singing and dancing a whole story of courtship, marriage and childbirth. It was one of the times I felt a oneness (community) with the people. The singer was not young. The response to her was much deeper than to an entertainer. It was more as if she was saying, this is how it is: innocence, experience, pain, and joy. It was a very open sharing of experience, that isn't a normal part of our own cultural experience.

Conflict with tradition is sometimes the result of education. My surface observations revealed such situations. Education was seen as the great need and the government's main efforts were toward building schools and training teachers. The year I was there, the law provided that every child between six and nine years of age, who had not yet been admitted to grade one should have a place. The schools were having a difficult time making room for the great number who had until then been unable to gain admittance. Only half of those who qualified for secondary school found places. Some men had received college, university, or technical education in the U.K. or Europe. They had gone there for several years and their wives remained in Zambia. On returning, these men moved up socially and in government or civil service. The wife, not only had much less education than her husband, she also had no knowledge of the cultures he desired to emulate. These marriages had a low survival rate. Some of the younger women were better educated as they had been trained as secretaries for the new government. It is easy to see the upset in the traditional pattern where older women were respected by the younger ones. It is easy to imagine the confused inter-personal relations in a home where a child knows more than his parents who have been socialized in a traditional society.

The fact that English was chosen as the national language and is used in schools also confuses values. It was chosen to avoid friction among the tribes, if one of the more than eight major African languages spoken in the country had been chosen. The secondary education is all in English. Men who have worked for the British know English; women do not, except for the very young.

The government with concern for tradition has set-up a Department of Culture to preserve dances, music, dress, crafts, etc. The daily press is constantly calling on the older women to lecture the younger women about their dress and morals. It was suggested that a law be passed to jail the parents if an unmarried girl became pregnant. Advice given in an "Ann Landers" type column was often of the pattern, "go back to the village and ask your elders for guidance."

In traditional societies, it is not unusual for parents to retain some authority, even after the son or daughter marries. I had a friend from Kenya who was having marriage problems. She told me that her husband's parents were supposed to be intermediaries; to find out if her complaints were justified; if so, to pressure him to change his ways. She was an emotionally stable, educated, and mature person. Their oldest child was twelve, the youngest was two. She thought the two of them could work things out. Though the distance was great the husband's parents did intervene; and their official disapproval of his way of life seemed to have a lot of power, even in what appeared to be, a modern marriage. When I left, they seemed to have solved their problems.

The implications are easier to see in another culture, but seeing patterns there makes it easier to see something similar in our own. As people get older they are no longer considered wiser or as having something valuable to offer the young.

Respect and dignity are two words one quickly associates with the people, but in another situation, where I had become a part of the system, there was a different impression. Food was expensive. The basic diet of maize meal, fixed as a porridge for breakfast; and for the main meal, nshima was made by cooking the maize meal thick enough to be rolled with the fingers into small balls which could then be dipped in a sauce. In some fortunate rural areas where there were fish or small game or ground nuts available, the diet contained sufficient protein. In the city where protein is expensive diets were not adequate.

I belonged to the Ndola Nutrition Group which made an effort to obtain protein in bulk at the best bargain price possible and then to package it in small amounts and sell at cost. I went with a Zambian lady twice a week to the Itawa clinic on the outskirts of Ndola. The time had been set aside to examine pre-school children and it seemed the best time to contact mothers in order to sell small packets of dried fish, milk biscuits, ground nuts, dried beans, milk powder and, sometimes, tinned meats and fish were available. My husband was working with poultry farmers so I made arrangements to get eggs twice a week. These could be sold more cheaply than the going rate, and we limited each purchase to one dozen eggs, so that the supplies would go around. First, we gave a short presentation over a charcoal burner, then we would sell whatever we had brought. When we first started selling eggs it was a mob scene; young women with babies on their backs, children, and old woman all tried to get theirs first as they feared that there would not be enough for all. There was no respect for age or infirmity, and I was just another marketer. When our little table was in danger of collapsing and we were jammed against the wall, the medical technician in charge of the clinic, took us and our products inside; from there, we could sell through a small window. In such a situation respect for age or wisdom disappears, as does consideration for the young and the weak.

Marketers in the township markets are usually middle-ages women who are trying to get every ngwe they can to support their families. Sometimes the daily press would speak out about their unscrupulous practices. One day one of these lady entrepreneurs came to our house because we had avocados to give away. We had two huge trees with fruit the size of grapefruit. The ladies seemed to be a mother and daughter. They filled two huge burlap bags. Then with babies on their backs they started to put the bags of avocados on their heads. It was a three-mile walk to their home and one lady was already starting down the drive with the heavy load, when Les offered them a ride in the car. The older lady was a marketer who would sell the avocados for 5 or 10 ngwee (7-14 cents) at the local market and seemed to me that she had earned every penny.

Les said that in many of the poultry farms he worked with, it was the older women who were involved in commercial poultry ventures. His most frightening experience was when he first arrived in Ndola and was taken to visit Kafubu, a cooperative village. There had been some confusion about the payments due from egg sales and he was introduced to the village by being met by a group of angry righteous women waving their hands and yelling. They stopped the car, in which he was riding, with the Zambian poultry technician and the manager of the co-op. The men were too frightened to give the women an audience and made a hasty retreat. The problem was solved later.

A stay in a hospital was an opportunity for me to be close to the 'Zambian women. I couldn't speak Cibemba, but in the large ward we smiled at each other and in our common suffering seemed to communicate. The lady next to me was middle-aged and, I think, she must have been someone important in her village. When the door opened at noon for the visiting hour, eleven persons, mostly men, came in and stood by her bed. They came in silently and greeted her with a clap-clap of the hands, then touching their hearts. Their motions were full of feeling. They looked closely and respectfully at the bottle of plasma and their eyes followed the tube which connected with her arm. No words were exchanged. I don't know whether they were persons who in ordinary life would not have conversed or whether they were awed with the power of the modern mutei (the word medicine is the same as the word for tree). When the time was up they left silently. They conveyed to me a deep feeling for the lady in the bed and even more than that; an awe for the life and death processes that were happening.

I would like to draw this together in some definite, concise way, but I realize these impressions are like a patchwork, which has meaning only for the person who remembers where each piece came from. This is the first time I have tried to think of our life in Zambia, in relation to aging. The conflict between traditional life and new government, technology, and economy were impressions we were always aware of. In retrospect, it is easy to see that the changing society is causing a change in the attitudes toward the old.

Patricia Hernan Grube from a class at UCSC, 1976

Note: McLuhan coined the expression "the medium is the message" and the term global village, and predicted the World Wide Web almost thirty years before it was invented. He was a fixture in media discourse in the late 1960s, though his influence began to wane in the early 1970s. ~ Wikipedia

About the author . . .

Patricia Hernan Grube is a playwright and poet from Santa Cruz. Born in the desert of Arizona, she moved with her family to California when she was eleven. Her education at UC Berkley was interrupted during World War II. Later she received degrees in Sociology and Psychology from UC Santa Cruz. Her work seeks to find drama and transcendence in the lives of ordinary people. She is most proud of her talented family.

Her books of poetry are: *The Green Door, Layer by Layer* and *Then and Now*. Some of her plays that have been produced include: *Grandpa's Breakfast, Falling Apples, Found Wanting, Relative Shades, Blue, Nshima* and *Twilight*.

Nshima was based on some of her memories of time spent in Zambia. In 2014 she wrote some stories about those memories. When they were done, she asked the rest of the family to also write a memory. Included in the book is a tape where Lester shares his work.